Dance of the Rainmaker

SUMMIT LEARNING SYSTEMS

Dance of the Rainmaker

CREATING AUTHENTIC DIFFERENTIATION
IN TODAY'S COMPETITIVE MARKETPLACE

Michael Vickers

SUMMIT
LEARNING SYSTEMS

Summit Press

A Division of Summit Learning Systems, Inc.

Suite #1719, 246 Stewart Green SW,

Calgary, Alberta T3H 3C8

This book may be purchased for educational, business, or sales
promotional use at special quantity discounts to use as premiums
and sales promotions or for use in corporate training programs.

For information call: 888-817-3751

Visit our Website at www.michaelvickers.com

Design and Production: David Counsell

Editing: David Counsell

Copy Editing: Beth Smith and Tori Smith

Printed and Bound in the United States of America

First Printing: August 2015

Second Printing

Third Printing

Fourth Printing

9 8 7 6 5 4 3 2 1

Library of Congress Cataloging-in-Publication Data

Vickers, Michael

Dance of the Rainmaker: Creating Authentic Differentiation in
Today's Competitve Marketplace /

Michael Vickers.

p. cm.

ISBN 978-0-9713250-1-2

This book is dedicated to my beautiful wife
and best friend, Beth and to our seven
amazing children – Ashley, Scott, Kendra,
Lesley, Tori, Scott and Kelsey –
who give meaning to what we do.

Acknowledgments

Projects like *Dance of the Rainmaker* don't come easily to me. While I love to present and share strategies and tactics with my live audiences, putting it all down on paper in a linear way for a book represents a real challenge. I'm grateful to those who have helped make this book a reality. It's the culmination of many wonderful years of experience working with top sales performers from myriad industries across North America. The real-world strategies and tactics presented here are a testament to the trust my clients have afforded me as we embarked on many varied and memorable journeys together. Without you, there is no book.

A special thanks to my wife, Beth and our daughter, Tori for their exceptional editing skills and to my research partner, creative director and sounding board, David Counsell at Ideamax Consulting Group. All of your efforts and skills are very much appreciated. Together you've made me look much better than I could ever have done on my own.

Thank you one and all.

Table of Contents

Acknowledgments 7

Chapter 1: Becoming the Emotional Favorite 11

Chapter 2: Building Relationships 21

Chapter 3: Value Matters 32

Chapter 4: Value-Added Positioning 46

Chapter 5: Creating Distinctive Value 62

Chapter 6: The Sales Process 83

Chapter 7: The Question Protocol 104

Chapter 8: Handling Buyer Resistance 130

Chapter 9: Target Niche Marketing 137

Chapter 10: Selling to the C-Suite 150

Chapter 11: The 21st Century Time System 172

Final Thoughts 188

CHAPTER 1

Becoming the Emotional Favorite

In today's increasingly crowded marketplace, you need to stand apart from your competitors if you want to enjoy market differentiation and long-term success. You *must* become the preferred vendor in the eyes of your customers. And in this book, we'll show you how to do just that – how to become preferred by becoming the emotional favorite of your customers. To begin your journey to becoming the emotional favorite, you need to have a really strong understanding of what drives today's marketplace and what really matters, because it may be a bit different than you currently think. So let's start with getting to know how the marketplace really works.

The Revenue Ladder

Let's face it, at some level, everyone works for the money. We may love what we do, but our love affair wouldn't last very long if we weren't compensated for it. Now, the exact level of compensation is different from job to job, from person to person. If we picture revenue levels as rungs on a ladder, we can see that there's quite a difference between the top rung and the bottom one. Our ladder can represent personal income, or it might be corporate revenues; the metaphor works either way.

At the top of the revenue ladder, there are professionals that make literally millions of dollars per year or sometimes even hundreds of

millions of dollars. They might include movie stars, athletes, enter-
tainers, talk show hosts and corporate executives. At the top is the
rare air that, unfortunately, very few of the working population ever
get to breathe.

At the opposite end of the spectrum – the bottom of the revenue
ladder – we have people who make only minimum wage, struggling
to make ends meet with fewer choices and even less flexibility. Then
we have everyone in between.

Each of us, as a working professional, occupies a rung somewhere
on the ladder. I think it's pretty safe to say that most of us would
be delighted to climb up the ladder from our current position. Who
among us wouldn't like to move up to greater levels of reward for
the services we provide to the marketplace? When I ask audiences if
they think they're getting paid what they're worth, I usually hear a
resounding chorus of *NOs!*

So if we think we're worth more than we're currently getting paid,
the first thing we should be asking ourselves is, "What's holding us
back?" Why do some people move up the ladder so effortlessly and
get paid obscene amounts of money while others who work just as
hard or in many cases much harder, just can't achieve any momentum
or growth?

How the Marketplace Works

Here's the reality of today's marketplace. The marketplace doesn't
care how smart you are. It doesn't care how well intentioned you
are. It doesn't care if you're black or white or green or somewhere in
between! It doesn't care if you're male or female; young or old.

What the marketplace *does* care about is how much *value* you bring
to it. The more value you bring to the marketplace, the more it will
reward you. This applies to individuals, companies and organizations.
The hard truth of the marketplace is that your current rung on the revenue ladder is directly proportionate to the value you're bringing to

the marketplace. And here's the key: *as the marketplace defines the value;* not as you define it. It doesn't matter what you think. Right or wrong, the marketplace is the only true arbiter of value. This concept is often difficult for many people to accept, but you'll never break through your current revenue ceilings until you understand that this is just the way it is.

Rare, Precious & Unique

The marketplace *will* pay a premium for what it perceives to be rare, precious and unique. And the problem for many people and organizations is that they are none of those things. If you're not getting paid what you're worth, then the market does not perceive your service as rare enough, precious enough or unique enough. Here's a good test: is the value you bring to your company so special that you're being talked about and noticed by others outside your company? Do you have other employers calling you with better offers for your services? Does your employer have to fight to keep you? If not, then you're probably making exactly what you're worth – at least in the eyes of the marketplace. It may not always seem fair, but again, that's just the way the market works.

Free Agency

Think about it for a moment – in sports it's called free agency. Teams actively bid against one another for players they perceive to be of higher value. This kind of payment protocol is seen in the entertainment business as well. In the movies, the bigger the box-office draw, the more an actor or actress will get paid. In business, a company that provides a product or service of perceived higher value will command a higher price. When a product is deemed precious and unique, people will often enthusiastically pay a higher price and sometimes even line up overnight to be among the first to purchase. That's exactly what happens when Apple releases a new iPhone.

Moving Up the Ladder

When we start to understand how the market defines value, then we can start increasing the value we provide and begin moving up the revenue ladder. It also helps to understand that factors you may consider highly important are not always viewed that way by the market. Let's look at some examples.

Time

Many sales professionals wanting to earn more think that if they just put in more time they'll move up the revenue ladder. But time is a limiting factor because it's a finite resource. The average sales professional has only about 40-60 hours per week in which he or she will be productive. Over the long haul, this level of commitment is difficult to sustain and often leads to burnout. Most business executives have about 2000 hours in their year and putting in an extra 100 or so really won't make that much of a difference. If you're compensated by the hour, it's even harder. Your income will be capped by the amount of hours you are able to work. Either way, just putting in more time is not a very efficient way to move up the revenue ladder.

Education

Some sales professionals believe that if they could just get a better education they'd be able to move up the revenue ladder. This is sometimes true, providing that it's the right kind of education, but not always. Let's do a little comparison exercise.

Think of the education level required to be a university professor. Now, approximate in your mind what rung university professors might occupy on the revenue ladder. Next, let's take a look at professional athletes today and their positions on the revenue ladder. It quickly becomes exceedingly clear that professional athletes, regardless of their education level, are often valued very differently than our most educated university professors.

That's not to say that education is not valuable. Applicable, specialized education will definitely help us move up the revenue ladder, but by itself, it has its limits. The marketplace values relevant education and leading-edge knowledge that is utilized to create new, rare, precious and unique products and services. To make education really work in your favor, you must be able to apply it differently than your competitors and you must be committed to continuous improvement. Be prepared to constantly upgrade your knowledge base in order to sustain your relevance and be in a position to create the next new, rare, precious and unique product or service. Remember, we paid $1000 for the very first VCRs, but now they're virtually worthless. They were made obsolete by the DVD. The DVD player has almost been completely replaced by Blu-Ray technology which is now being supplanted by on-demand digital streaming. And so it goes.

Social Factors

There may have been a time in the past when your earning potential could be influenced by such social factors as gender, age and ethnicity, but in today's sophisticated modern marketplace, they hold very little influence, if any at all. Women have crashed the executive suite and the corridors of power. Today's technology-savvy youth have made the Internet their playground for a whole new world of wealth generation. The presidency of the United States is no longer restricted by a color barrier. Today's marketplace has evolved in dramatic fashion. What matters is ability, creativity, speed and follow-through. The marketplace doesn't care where the idea comes from; it just cares about the *value* of the idea. Value talks, everything else walks. Value is what's relevant.

It's About What You Bring

The bottom line is that your movement up the revenue ladder has everything to do with the quantity and quality of the value you bring to the market. As the market defines that value! The secret then is to understand what the market values and how you can provide that value. My goal with this book is to provide you with strategies and tactics that, if you'll apply consistently, will increase your own distinctive value and uniqueness and help you move up the revenue ladder.

Understanding Agendas

When you work for an organization, you have to realize that it has a very specific agenda. In almost every case, its primary goal is to make a profit for its stakeholders. Profit is the reason for its existence. The goals and objectives of the organization may not always exactly reflect the goals of its employees, but as long as the agenda of each party can serve the other, a relationship will exist.

Understanding this basic underlying concept is an important element of learning how to become the emotional favorite. People, organizations and corporations all have their own agendas; it's just how we operate. And when you understand the other person's agenda, the rest of the process is quite simple. Our goal as sales professionals is to determine what the agendas of our customers are and then do everything we can to make sure our solutions help them meet those agendas. The question categories we'll explore in the upcoming *Question Protocol* chapter will assist you in developing the types of questions that will help you determine your clients' agendas. When you know your clients' agendas and what represents the greatest value to them, you're in the driver's seat.

Your goal in the marketplace is to become the preferred provider of what you sell. Preferred means first choice; customers would rather deal with you than any of your competitors because you've established yourself as the emotional favorite. And when you become preferred, you have much better insulation against competitive erosion.

Make no mistake, whether you're #1 or #10 in your industry, the competition is always trying eat your lunch. If we think of the marketplace as a pie, and assume that you have an industry leading 15%

market-share, that still means that 85% of the market is trying to take business away from you – they're trying to eat your lunch. When business is good and the whole market pie is expanding, then your portion of the pie grows just by virtue of being in an expanding market. On the other hand, if industry sales are shrinking, then the only way you can grow is at the expense of another competitor. Insulating yourself against competitive forces helps to protect your customer base and best of all, your margins. Preferred vendors enjoy higher margins because they don't have to compete on price nearly as much as the competitors that are chasing them.

Challenging Assumptions

If we want to blow through our income ceilings we really need to take a close look at the assumptions we make... assumptions about our customers, our competitors and ourselves. Our assumptions guide our actions and our actions determine our results. If our assumptions are wrong, the results could potentially be devastating. My job is to challenge some of the assumptions you may have about selling. Most sales professionals rarely look at their practice from an outside perspective, from the 30,000 foot level, and as a result they often miss relevant details that impact their results. My intention is to challenge any traditional assumptions you may have about positioning value, how you approach selling and how to differentiate yourself from your competition.

One of the first assumptions salespeople make is about the motivation behind a customer's purchasing decision. They assume that their clients are buying from a logical perspective. They think that because the purchase is business-related that it's a clear-cut case of what makes the most sense logically. Emotion shouldn't enter the picture. Well, sorry to say – this is a big mistake! People are people. Whether they purchase for personal or business reasons, people make their purchasing decisions based on *both* logic and emotion. Most of the time, they buy first for emotional reasons and then rationalize the emotional decision with logic. Even though it may seem to go against the grain in a business environment, you can bank on it being consistent and predictable purchasing behavior.

How are We Selling?

So the question you need to ask yourself is, "How am I selling? Emotionally or logically?" Most salespeople are in fact selling logically because of the chaotic nature of today's business environment. They'll go out of their way to highlight the strength of their carefully assembled quantitative data in order to support the proposed solution. Although this is a critical part of the process and our product or service must represent a viable solution in the minds of customers, ultimately it's not the determining factor in their decision-making process.

Think of it this way. You have a killer solution; it meets all the customer's essential criteria and even goes beyond to provide extra value that the competition either didn't think of or cannot provide. Sounds like a slam dunk, doesn't it? But there's a catch – the customer doesn't really like you personally. Nothing concrete – just an irrational, "can't really explain it" kind of thing. But he really likes your competitor, even though their solution is not as strong as yours. Who do you think is going to win the business? If customers don't like you, they won't buy from you. Simple as that. They'll find a way to rationalize going with your competitor. They'll invent some sort of logical reason to justify a totally emotional decision.

Don't worry, it's happened to the best of us. But the key from here forward is that you shouldn't be letting it happen again. *Dance of the Rainmaker* will show you how to position yourself as the emotional favorite, how to identify the customer's buying triggers and then fully leverage them.

Stress for Success

Everyone knows the old adage, "dress for success", but I think the key to success is really all about *stress*; learning to understand and embrace stress. It's a well known fact that we're all stressed out to one degree or another. It could be work-related stress, or personal stress; it doesn't matter. The fact is that, for human beings, stress is a part of daily life. And boy, are our customers ever stressed out! They've got challenges and issues coming at them from all angles and the chaos and speed of change in today's marketplace is ramping up stress levels to all-time highs. Our ability as sales and service organizations to correctly identify the key stresses of our customers and to eliminate or mitigate those stresses through our business processes, in a better way than our competitors, will have a huge impact on who our customers choose to do business with.

This book will teach you how to identify the key stresses your client may be experiencing and how to provide solutions that will make those stresses go away or at the very least mitigate their impact.

The road to becoming preferred and the emotional favorite is really quite clear. You will become the preferred provider if you can successfully accomplish 3 things:

1. *Identify your customer's stress and dissatisfaction better than the competition.*
2. *Remove your customer's stress and dissatisfaction better than the competition.*
3. *Connect with your customers in a meaningful way.*

At this point you should know that no matter where you are on the revenue ladder, the only way up is to provide more value to the marketplace as the marketplace determines that value. You need to find out what your customers value most; what their individual and corporate agendas are. You must then leverage that knowledge by identifying and eliminating their key stresses and dissatisfaction factors. Finally, you have to bring it all together by forging strong emotional connections.

What's Next

In our next chapter we delve into the two distinct types of selling and which one you're most likely to be utilizing as a professional salesperson. I'll show you a model for understanding how relationships work in the selling process and what you need to focus on if you're going to rise above and stand out from your competiton.

We'll explore customer expectations and why what you may think is a compelling competitive advantage is not viewed that way by your customers.

CHAPTER 2

Building Relationships

There are basically two types of selling situations. One simple, the other much more detailed and complex. The simple situation is the straight transaction. When you log on to Amazon.com and choose the book you want to buy, you put it in your cart and proceed to the checkout. There is no personal interaction and the process is very straightforward. You know what you want and you buy it. It's easy and convenient and requires virtually no assistance.

Relationship Selling

The other type of selling situation is one that involves personal interaction between the buyer and seller in order to confirm and complete the sale. A relationship of some sort must be established. And it's your approach to this relationship-based selling situation that will either bring you the rewards and glory of success or relegate you to the *same as all the rest* scrap heap of mediocrity. That may sound a bit dramatic, but it's true. Your sales success is directly proportionate to your ability to build great relationships. Building a great relationship is just like building a house – you have to start with a strong foundation. And with relationships, that foundation, from which everything else arises, is **trust**. You can have a business relationship without trust, but it won't be built to last. You'll eventually lose out to one where trust exists.

So it follows that it's essential to build trusting relationships if you want to enjoy long-term success. But building trust can be a time-consuming affair. The question to ask yourself as a sales professional is, *"How can I build a relationship of trust quickly?"* The ability to build trust quickly equates to more sales and more rewards so that's where we are going to continue our journey forward.

The Relationship Model

Let's begin by visualizing a model for relationships as being a pie split into three sections. On the bottom third of the pie, forming the foundation, is *Trust*. The next third of the pie is what I refer to as *High Task*. High Task is comprised of all the core competencies you bring to the relationship. It's what you and your company actually do – whatever service or product you provide. These High Task competencies are the primary drivers for getting customers interested in the first place. The High Task part of the model is all about ensuring that your products or services meet the basic needs and expectations of your customers. Think of it as your core competency. Let's examine the concept of High Task a bit further before we move on to the final third of the model.

Basic Expectations

In today's marketplace, customers expect us to listen to their needs, provide solutions that make sense and do what we say we're going to do. These are their basic expectations. It's important to note here that we never exceed their expectations when we do what we say we're going to do. Doing what we say we're going to do is simply meeting the customer's most basic level of expectation.

As a sales professional, it's a good idea to be asking yourself the following question. *"Why should the customer do business with me?"*

Here's what I often hear from sales professionals in response to that question:

"We're competitive."

"We have great quality solutions."

"We listen to the needs of our customers."

"We have great delivery options."

"We have a great selection."

"We have customization options."

"We guarantee our service."

"We are number one in our markets."

Sound familiar? Now let's look closely at each of these typical responses and ask ourselves this question. *"Am I meeting or exceeding the customers expectations when I provide these things?"*

The truth is that, in most cases, these are expectations that customers have right from the start. By doing these, you're just meeting basic expectations.

Now let's suppose that we bring in your competition and pose the same question, *"Why should the customer buy from you?"* There's a really good chance we're going to hear all the same responses regardless of whether they're true or not. Now bring in the next competitor and the next and so on and so on. The story remains the same. You soon start to realize that companies *have* to offer these basic elements. It's what they have to do just to compete in the game. High Task competencies are the functional and logical part of the Relationship Model. They're essential, but they're not special.

The Final Component

Now let's look at the third and final component of the three-part Relationship Model. This final third of our model has less to do with tangible product features and benefits and more to do with *intangibles* such as service and personal relationships. It represents the emotional component of the relationship. These are things we call *High Touch*. The things that make your customers feel special and really appreciated. High Touch is all about the things we do that allow us to exceed our customers' expectations.

Now ask yourself the following question, *"What do you do to exceed your customer's expectations?"* What do you do that makes them go, *"Wow, I sure didn't expect that!"*? And here's where it gets really interesting. The strategic mistake many sales professionals make is that they believe the marketplace is judging them solely against the competition within their own industry. Consciously this might make sense, but unconsciously your customer is really judging you by whoever is providing the best experience and highest level of service in business today, regardless of the industry.

Providing High Touch offerings also has a nice effect on your margins. Think for a moment of the companies that are known internationally for their exceptional service. Companies like Four Seasons, Jet Blue, Southwest Airlines, FedEx, Disney, Starbucks, Apple, etc. Now the next question to ask is, "Do you ever ask them for a discount?" You might try but High Touch leaders rarely have to discount to get the business.

The lesson for Rainmakers is to simply look at the best in business today, regardless of the industry, and then look at where your business is in comparison. The difference between your offering and theirs is what I call the gap. The goal then is to try your best to close the gap wherever possible. Now here's the bad news. Companies like those we've just mentioned will probably stay ahead of you on the *High Touch* side of the business because that's where they focus. Don't worry about being better than them, just try to model yourself after them. What you're essentially doing is looking beyond the standards of your own industry and evaluating the best in business today, regardless of industry. The goal is to then incorporate the best practices you discover into your business. More than likely, your competition won't be doing this; they'll simply be watching what their own industry is doing!

Rules for Exceeding Expectations

If our goal then is to exceed customer expectations, there are two simple rules that will help guide you and keep you focused on what is most important to customers.

Rule #1: Take a standard service offering and up-level it

Carefully examine all of your service offerings and look for ways to make them a little better. To take them beyond the expected to the unexpected, to the higher ground of *unique*. As we've discussed before, the marketplace rewards what is rare, unique and precious so that's what you should be striving for.

Let's say that after a major transaction you typically send out a thank you note or card to your customers thanking them for the business. Well, as you might guess, so do many other businesses. This is a basic core competency – saying thank you for the business – and your customers have grown to expect it. And when it's expected, it's really High Task rather than High Touch. So how can we up-level the concept of the thank you card to the point where it does becomes unexpected?

An Unexpected Twist

Let's suppose that you land a new account on July 1st. During the course of the year, you send out a few thank you notes after making sales and your customer is happy with your products and service. One year later on July 1st, why not send out an anniversary acknowledgment? For big customers you could do big things and for little customers you could do little things; whatever you deem to be appropriate.

The key is that most customers would not be expecting an anniversary acknowledgment – in fact they probably wouldn't even remember the date they started doing business with you. But the fact that y*ou* remembered is special. It's different and unexpected. It might be a simple card thanking them for the business over the past year. It might be sending in pizza for their entire staff. Whatever it is, the key is that it was triggered by their anniversary which is what makes it unexpected. If you're saying thanks in a way that's unique and your competition isn't, then you've just created a *WOW* moment. You've taken a simple High Task concept and up-leveled it to make it High Touch. And that's the kind of *High Touch* added value that can separate you from the competition.

Rule #2: Become a hero to the people you serve

When you do something that's in the best interest of the people you serve rather than your own, you become a hero in their eyes. Try looking at things more from the customers' viewpoint. What would make their jobs easier? More efficient? More exciting? More fun? What would make them feel special? There are so many opportunities to become a hero to your customers and you'll start to see them open up if you begin with that goal in mind. Once you tune in to becoming a hero to the people you serve, you can move to the next level which is *"How can I make the people I serve become heroes to the people that they serve?"* If you can make customers look good to their colleagues, their bosses, their friends, spouses, etc., then you'll really start to become preferred in their minds.

Let's imagine that you had identified that one of the stresses your customer was facing was how to fairly and efficiently evaluate similar products for different vendors. Perhaps this customer was not as experienced as he would like to be and he was nervous that his inexperience might inadvertently cause him to make the wrong decision. In this case, perhaps you could use your own knowledge and expertise to create an evaluation matrix that included all the features required and all pertinent questions that needed to be asked in order to make an informed decision. If it wasn't self-serving and was truly in the best interests of your client, this would go a long way to making you a hero in the eyes of the client. And even better, let's say that the client was then able to introduce this evaluation matrix to the rest of his purchasing colleagues for use throughout the company. This would certainly make him look good in their eyes and now you're an even bigger hero to your customer.

Remember, if you serve your customers and their needs first – before your own – you're on your way to becoming the emotional favorite.

Understanding how the relationship model works is an important part of your journey to becoming preferred and establishing trust as quickly as possible. Trust is your foundation, so creating trust is essential for everything else to work. From there, the key is to understand the difference between *High Task* and *High Touch* and how to create more high touch moments than your competition. A good rule of thumb here to help you determine between the two is, if it has anything to do with your core competency then you probably ought to be doing it. If it has nothing to do with your core competency, and everything to do with your client or customer, then you are exceeding expectations and creating High Touch.

Understanding Preferred

The best way to explain the concept and enable you to remember it, is to express it as a simple formula. So for all you math lovers out there, here's my formula for becoming preferred:

(EV + DV) x T = PS

Which is short for:

(Expected Value + Distinctive Value) x Trust = Preferred Status

To fully understand it, we need to break down the formula into individual components. Let's start with EV or Expected Value. This is just as the name implies – the value the customer expects to receive from you. It is, in essence, the *High Task* portion of the Relationship Model. In today's marketplace, customers expect quality products, they expect courteous service, they expect to be listened to, and they expect prompt delivery. These high tasks or expected values are the price of admission just to play in the game of business today.

Distinctive Value or DV is what makes you unique; it's what makes you rare or precious. This is the *High Touch* component of the Relationship Model. The marketplace will pay a premium for things they see as rare or unique. Becoming unique and rare should be the goal of every sales organization and if you are going to become a Rainmaker, then it is a top priority. This is a big topic that requires further discussion and we'll go into much greater detail on this subject in a forthcoming chapter entitled *Creating Distinctive Value*.

Next in our formula is the T and the T stands for *Trust*. Trust is the multiplier. The more the customer or prospect trusts you, the more business they will give you. It's quite common for today's customer to spread the business among a number of qualified vendors. They don't put all their eggs in one basket. Research shows however, that the vendor the customer trusts the most is the one who will win the majority of that customer's business.

So when you take your *Expected Value*, add to it your *Distinctive Value* and then multiply it all by *Trust*, the final result is *Preferred Status*.

The 3 Levels of Preferred Status

Preferred Status is not a singular outcome. There are three distinct levels to *Preferred Status* and understanding the differences is what really separates the market leaders.

Level #1 – Loyalty

The first level of preference is loyalty. Loyalty is almost always a highly sought-after commodity for sales organizations, but many surveys reveal that customer loyalty is often fickle and can easily be bought. When I ask people if they consider themselves to be loyal employees to their organizations, they almost always say yes. But when

I ask the same people if they would be interested in joining the competition for a 50% raise in salary and benefits, and I press them to be honest, most say that they would seriously consider jumping ship to the competition. This is why many competitors use price as an offensive weapon in order to win the business and then gradually increase prices over time to recapture profits. So loyalty is good, but it can be bought and it only represents the first level of preference. Instead we should be trying to move our loyal customers to the next level of *Preferred Status*.

Level #2 – Advocacy

Advocacy is when your customer base likes your product or service so much, they're willing to recommend you to others. They help do your marketing for you. They in fact become enthusiastic advocates for your products or service. This is why the *High Touch* strategy is so effective; it gets people talking about you. It's interesting to note that when you do what you say you are going to do – you meet their basic expectations – customers don't advocate for you. But when you exceed their expectations with *High Touch* offerings, they're delighted to share their experience with others.

Here's an example of how a *High Touch* strategy can create customer advocacy:

Several years ago, I was visiting a major city in North America and needed a taxi from the airport to a downtown hotel. The regulated price or fare as dictated by the meter and municipality said it would be a $50.00 flat rate for the fare. Anyone who has experienced taxi service understands that there is no room for negotiation on a regulated flat-rate fare.

When I got into the taxi, the first thing I noticed was how wonderfully clean and tidy it was inside. The driver greeted me and then asked me if I would like a Starbucks coffee before we started. On the front seat of the taxi was an egg crate with two thermoses of Starbucks coffee – one regular and one decaf. His timing couldn't have been better and I agreed to a regular coffee. He then offered me a piece of fruit or muffin to go with my coffee. Everything looked appetizing so I agreed to a muffin. He then held up three morning papers, one local and two national, for me to choose from. I grabbed the USA Today and started into my breakfast.

Now let's stop for a moment and take a look at how much he has invested in this experience. The coffee, piece of fruit and muffin are about a buck or two. The newspapers stay in the vehicle. So at this point, he hasn't really had to invest too much in creating a very pleasant *High Touch* offering that was quite different than what I had anticipated.

We arrived at my destination and the driver asked me if I came to visit this city often. I replied that I did, several times a month in fact. He then proceeded to tell me that when he goes to the airport to pick up a fare, it could sometimes involve up to a three hour wait. Sometimes the fare's final destination is an hour away and sometimes it's only a few minutes. It's sort of hit or miss as to whether his day is profitable or not.

But this is where he showed his true entrepreneurial spirit. He said that if I would simply contact him in advance of arriving in the city, by telephone, email or text, he would respond right away to confirm pick-up and under the taxi statutes, he could then wait at the curb with a sign with my name on it, effectively making the trip a charter. This way he could offer me the same level of service each time I came to his city.

Now let's think about this for a moment. The price is the same for all taxis, however with this provider, the experience is different. Given a choice, which one would you choose? And what do you think his tip revenue would be like at the end of the year compared to other taxi drivers?

It's what you add to the basic commodity that makes it unique and different from the competition. Once we have our clients advocating for us, we can then move them to the top level of *Preferred Status*.

Level #3 – Insistence

This is the ultimate level of preference. It's the promised land for Rainmakers and sales organizations. Insistence is just as the term implies. Customers enjoy doing business with you so much that they insist on dealing with you; they won't make a move without you. They're locked in and won't consider anyone else. I'm sure we all know people or companies that, at one time or another, have fit into this category for us. There are people who wouldn't consider any other computer than a Mac or any other smart phone than an iPhone. People who wouldn't drink any other cola than Coke. People who would only buy a Toyota and only from a specific salesperson at a specific dealership. When you attain this level of preference, you're much more insulated against the pressures of competition and downward pricing.

But don't ever forget that when you reach this level of preference, the expectations of your customers are very high. You should never take this positioning for granted. To stay there, you have to continually add to the experience, because your competitors will be playing copycat sooner or later. Customers will forgive minor slip-ups from people and companies that they insist on, but if you ignore them or don't work hard to keep making the experience of dealing with you better, eventually they'll be asking themselves, *"So what have you done for me lately?"* There used to be millions of people who insisted on GM cars. Nothing else would do. Not so much anymore.

What's Next

Coming up in our next chapter, we'll look at the concept of value and why it should be a key focal point for all your sales efforts. In addition, you'll discover what *currencies* affect your customers' buying decisions and how you can leverage each one to customize your approach to your customers' specific priorities.

CHAPTER 3

Value Matters

In this chapter, we're going to look at how you can deliberately and systematically increase the perception of total value to your customers. When you have a solid understanding of how to position your product or service from a value perspective, you'll be much better equipped to offset competitive pressure and be far less influenced by market demand to reduce your pricing.

As sales professionals, life would be so much easier for us if our customers inherently knew and appreciated how much value our products and services truly represented to them. Unfortunately, that's rarely the case. In today's marketplace, with the variety of options available to customers, it's wishful thinking to expect them to spend the time on their own to learn and understand how our offerings differ from those of the competition. In fact, customers often group suppliers of similar products or services together by default, thinking that everyone's version is pretty much the same. The problem with this scenario is that when all suppliers are viewed as providing essentially the same product or service, price becomes the point of differentiation in the customer's mind. If your response to this line of thinking is to lower your price to match a customer's demand, you end up serving no one; not yourself or the customer.

The key to long-term success is to adopt the philosophy of total value as a way to educate your customer base; to help them make better purchasing decisions and to increase your own profitability. When you position your products or services from a value perspective, not only are you employing a mutually beneficial win-win strategy, you're also effectively positioning yourself as more knowledgeable and professional than your competition.

The 5 Customer Currencies

In order for you to effectively create a superior solution for your customers, you really have to know what they value. When you know what's most important to them, you can focus your efforts much more effectively. I often refer to these values as *currencies* and it's essential to understand that there are at least five values or currencies that you can use to create stronger relationships. Unfortunately, many sales professionals only use the currency of money in their selling efforts and often they find themselves discounting in order to get the business. Rainmakers use all five currencies to provide maximum value to their customers. Let's take a look at the five currencies and see how we can apply them.

Currency #1 – Money

The first currency that most sales professionals are familiar with is money. Money represents the price of our product or service. Price is often used as the offensive weapon of choice when the competition is trying to take business away from us. We see constant downward pressure that in many cases is initiated by the salesperson trying to get the business rather than the customer requesting it. There is an important rule when it comes to money: *There can only be one price leader.*

Think about it for a moment. You're either the lowest cost provider or you're not. Now being the low cost provider is certainly an acceptable strategy, but it generally means that your margins are small. You have to operate your business with extreme efficiency to make up for low margins and you usually have to be big enough that you can make up the difference by scale. Being the low cost provider can be an effective strategy, just as being the premium cost provider can be effective. You just don't want to be in the middle because the middle is the death zone.

Think for a moment of the most expensive automobiles you can come up with. It's usually easy to name a few. Now name the cheapest. Again, this is a pretty easy exercise. Now comes the tricky part. Try listing the rest of the vehicles in the middle. And how is the middle of the pack faring these days? On last inspection many of those in this position are struggling to remain relevant.

The question sales professionals should always be asking is not *"What can we do to lower our prices to be more competitive?"*, but rather, *"What value must we start providing that the market will be willing to pay a premium for?"*

Value Conversations

A great strategy for dealing with the pricing issue is to initiate a conversation about value. I like to start a value conversation this way. *"Mr. Customer, are you looking for the cheapest acquisition cost or are you looking for the best total value solution?"* For some customers, it's only about price. The rule to remember here is that price is never the issue unless it *is* the issue and when it's the issue, it's the only issue! Survey after survey, however shows that price is rarely at the top of purchasing criterion. Here's the formula I use in my value conversations.

Acquisition Price + Maintenance + Impact = Total Value

Acquisition costs vary from time to time and only represent a portion of your total value. Maintenance refers to the costs over the lifetime of the product. Impact refers to how the product or service you're selling impacts the customer from a qualitative and quantitative perspective.

Let me give you an example.

Comparing Models

Let's say you're looking at purchasing a car and you're considering two different models. One is a $50,000 BMW and the other is a
$45,000 GM product. Which car represents the best value?

On first inspection, the GM product's *Acquisition Price* is $45,000,
which is $5,000 less than the BMW. So, if you're using acquisition
price as your only point of difference, the GM model wins. But let's
assume you've decided to employ the Value Formula here and you
move to the next factor in the equation – *Maintenance*. The BMW
has one of the industry's best five year bumper-to-bumper warranties,
while the GM warranty is not nearly as comprehensive. So when
considering the maintenance factor, the BMW would represent the
better value. But just for the sake of our example, let's assume both
cars have equal maintenance requirements; there's no real identifiable difference there. At this point, the GM would still represent the
better value because of its lower acquisition cost.

Now let's keep moving forward in the Total Value Formula and look
at the *Impact* variable. In five years, the BMW will be worth about
55-60% of it's original value; it has stronger residual market value and
is highly sought after among buyers as a previously owned vehicle.
Even at the low end of 55%, the BMW would bring back $27,500 to
the owner at the time of sale. That means the net cost of ownership of
the BMW over five years would be $50,000 minus $27,500 for a final
net figure of $22,500.

In five years, the GM product is worth 30-35% of the original value.
If we assume the high end of 35%, the GM would bring back $15,750
to the owner at the time of sale. So the net cost of ownership of the
GM over five years would be $45,000 minus $17,500 for a final net
figure of $27,500.

So just on that variable alone, over the five years of ownership, the

BMW becomes a better deal by at least $5000. The higher acquisition price is more than compensated for by the lower total cost of ownership.

The key takeaway here is that by disciplining yourself to the consistent utilization of the Total Value Formula, you'll be moving customers beyond the acquisition price variable and engaging them in a total value conversation which puts their best interests at the forefront of the purchasing experience.

Currency #2 – Time

The second customer currency is the currency of time. Will your customers pay a premium to save time? If so, how are you employing this currency?

The fact is that customers value time. FedEx charges a premium if you want next day delivery and they even offer different rates for different times throughout the day. Airlines work the same way. If you want to fly across the country this afternoon, you had better be prepared to pay a hefty premium. When it's really important, customers often *will* pay a premium for prioritization. Are you employing this strategy in your offering?

If you call Dell computers and order a customized computer, that's just the first part of your transaction. You will then be offered choices of delivery and each option carries a designated premium based on your time requirements. So, the first part of the transaction is buying the computer and the second part is about how soon you want it. Both parts have a price.

My guess is that many of your customers call up at given times and request that you expedite delivery of your product or service. Are you extracting a premium or are you just giving it away? The challenge is that when you meet their request without the premium, customers will expect the same level of service the next time they order your product or service. If you simply let customers know that you offer a new expediting service but there is a premium to it, you will hear one of two responses from them:

"Great, please go ahead and send it" or... *"That's okay, let's just go ahead with your normal delivery times."*

If you're still having a challenge with charging your customer the time premium, then let them know there is one and what it is, but that you're willing to waive it because you truly appreciate their business. At least then, your customers know there's a specific value associated with the expedited delivery and they can tangibly see it as a value-added service. It also protects you against future requests, because they now realize there is a specific premium associated with faster delivery and that they may not automatically get it the next time.

Currency #3 – Prestige

Let's move on to our third currency prestige. Will your customers pay a premium to feel special?

You can buy a watch for $50 that tells you the time and date. You can also buy a watch for $5,000 dollars that tells you the time and date. $50 for the time and date function and $4,950 for the prestige of ownership!

Why do we drive what we drive? Why do we live where we live? Why do we wear what we wear? Make no mistake, prestige is a major influencer of our purchasing behavior.

Prestige is also about the power of your brand. If your brand is the market leader, then you will enjoy the currency of prestige. If you don't have the currency of prestige then you can always associate yourself with someone else's. Try taking your client for coffee at Starbucks or lunch at a trend-setting restaurant rather than less prestigious alternatives. This is why client outings such as major league sporting events or rounds of golf at high-end courses are popular among Rainmakers. Associating yourself with the prestige of other market leaders helps to position you as a prestigious provider as well.

Currency #4 – Reliability

The fourth currency is the currency of reliability. Will your customers pay a premium for reliability?

In many cases people will happily pay a premium for reliability. Most people realize that for a wide variety of products, the initial purchase price represents just one part of the total cost of ownership. The more reliable a product or service is, the lower the cost of maintenance will be over the lifetime of ownership. Why do Toyota and Honda automobiles always rank so high in customer surveys even though they often cost more than their direct competitors? Reliability is one of the main reasons.   Most people are willing to pay more up front if you can show them that the reliability of your product or service will end up meaning a lower total cost of ownership over a lifetime of use.

People inherently associate a higher cost with better quality and reliability. Rainmakers know that if they can quantify their product's quality, reliability or security, they can use it as a point of differentiation and extract a premium for it. If you can demonstrate how much it will cost a customer if an inferior product or service doesn't meet expectations and how your offering can out-last or stay in service longer, you can confidently justify a premium.

Currency #5 – Knowledge

The fifth currency is the currency of knowledge. Will your customers pay a premium for knowledge or wisdom? How are you employing this currency?

We started out in the Agricultural Age; we moved into the Industrial Age; then evolved into the Technology Age. Today there is a widespread consensus that we have moved into the Information Age. Will your customers pay a premium for information?

We will cover much more on this currency in our forthcoming chapter on *Creating Distinctive Value*, but the important point to remember with this currency is that when you partner with knowledge your value becomes distinctive.

Rainmakers understand that knowledge is a highly valuable currency and they employ it as often as they can. With today's business pressures and time constraints, most customers are either unable or unwilling to seek out and absorb all of the information and knowledge available to them in the marketplace to make the most informed choices. They end up relying on salespeople to filter this information and have to trust them to deliver the information which will be most applicable to their particular circumstances. Customers expect information, knowledge and wisdom as it relates to the product or service they're looking at purchasing, but it's a real surprise to receive valuable information from the salesperson that has nothing to do with the salesperson's product or service. Customers just naturally assume that most of the information provided by salespeople will be in the salesperson's best interest first and theirs second.

This is why employing the currency of knowledge can be so powerful. It gives salespeople an opportunity to significantly up-level the value they provide by delivering information that is not related to their product or service, but rather, related to the direct needs of the customer.

The rule of thumb here is simple – when the information or knowledge you are delivering is related in any way to your product or service, it's expected. When it has nothing to do with your product or service and everything to do with the customer's business, then you are exceeding expectations and setting yourself apart from the competition.

Here are a few examples of how Rainmakers use knowledge to differentiate themselves.

- They carry articles of interest from a wide variety of business magazines.
- They have several copies of the most talked about business books that they will leave with their best customers.

- They routinely send out information or updates on the latest technologies that look like they will be useful to their customers or become entrenched in their business cultures.

Anything that will enhance or improve business operations for customers or even enhance their personal lifestyles is fair game.

If the knowledge is useful to your customers and helps to relieve any of their stresses, whether it's business oriented or of a more personal nature, then you've created a WOW moment of extra value that will separate you from the pack. You've demonstrated in a very tangible fashion that you have their best interests at heart before your own.

To sum up, remember that there are 5 currencies you can employ. Whenever you're looking at making a real impact with your customers, try to leverage as many of these currencies as possible and you'll enjoy much greater success than those who simply focus on the price game.

The Value/Price Relationship

This *High Touch* strategy is effective because it leverages the underlying principles of the relationship between value and price. The Value/Price Relationship dictates that when you bring a small amount of value to the relationship, the price of doing business with you is big. If you're trying to take business away from an incumbent vendor and there is not enough perceived value in what you offer, then the inconvenience of switching to you is too great. Potential customers won't be willing to pull the trigger.

On the other hand, if you clearly offer higher value – as your prospects define value – then the perceived price of doing business with you is much less. Any inconvenience the customer might associate with making the change to your products or services will be significantly reduced because the value you bring is so high.

The Proper Balance

It is essential to work continuously at maintaining a healthy balance with your client relationships. A good metaphor for the Value/Price Relationship is a bank account. As with a bank account, a relationship grows stronger with regular deposits. If you're making more withdrawals than deposits and you run a deficit in your relationship account, then you're most likely on your way out, whether you know it or not. You never want your clients doing more for you than you are doing for them.

Just like personal relationships, business relationships tend to end when we take them for granted. You need to be really honest with yourself and ask, *"What have I really done lately for my best customers to show them that I appreciate their business and never take it or them for granted?"*

How many of your customers are staying with you only because it's too much of an inconvenience at the moment to change? Or perhaps it's because there isn't a viable alternative supplier yet. Do you really know or are you just making an assumption that no complaints means everything is fine?

Your Customer's Point System

Whether you realize it or not, your customers are keeping score when it comes to their business relationships. They have a point system they use to grade their relationships with suppliers. And it's not the same as your own system. They keep score differently than you do. What you may think of as high value, they may consider to be low value and so on. To truly insulate your clients from competitive erosion, it's essential to discover what they value. As sales professionals, we must fully understand their point system and treat them in the way they prefer to be treated. Even within the same industry, all clients are not equal.

Rainmakers that understand their client's point system and how to deliver value as their clients define it, enjoy market security and preferred status.

Attracting New Business

Let's take a moment and apply the Value/Price Relationship strategy to your new client attraction process.

If you've been in professional sales for any length of time, then you've undoubtedly made a sales call only to be told that the prospect is currently using your competitor and is quite happy with their services. In short, they're not interested in hearing your message. The prospect is not rejecting you personally, because they don't know you personally. The reason they feel comfortable sending you away is because you have not demonstrated anything that represents truly superior value to them. The pain of changing from an existing relationship is too great compared to any perceived benefits you might be able to show.

When the value you bring to the relationship is small, the price of doing business with you is too high.

But you shouldn't always take that first rejection at face value. If you're confident of the high value you offer in specific areas, you can politely probe the client as to his or her level of satisfaction in these particular areas. Many times clients assume that there's no difference between one supplier and the next, or that their current supplier is the best, because that's what he told them! Remember, clients are often too busy to make critical evaluations on their own. But if you can present the high value you bring in a way that's apparent, to be directly in your customers' best interests, then they're often open to a conversation. At the very least, you'll be planting a seed for the future and you've got their attention.

Remember that by simply being aware of how the Value/Price Relationship works, you can tailor your offering to be much more interesting and persuasive to potential customers.

The Second Place Strategy

I'm going to share with you one of my favorite strategies for landing new clients which clearly illustrates the Value/Price Relationship in action. First, we need to take a few steps back so that we can get on the same page. Let's assume that you have identified a potential opportunity that you're going to target. You make an appointment with the key decision maker, you develop some rapport, you further qualify them as a potential customer through some carefully crafted questions, prepare some customized solutions that look like a perfect fit and then get told by the customer that they already have a provider they're happy with and have been with them for years. Sound familiar? Let's look at what is really going on with the customer.

If customers are not initially interested in switching, you can safely assume the reason they said no was because there was not enough value in the relationship bank account to entice them to make a move. The pain of change was too much in relation to the value they see you bringing to the table. In other words, it's less painful for them to stay with status quo rather than switch to you. What they're really saying to you when they don't make a switch is that they don't trust you yet. Remember, trust is the foundation of all relationships.

When salespeople run into these types of situations and get a response from the customer such as, *"We are very happy with our current provider"* or, *"Our supplier has been with us for years and we don't see a need to switch"*, they often consider this an obstacle that will be difficult to overcome. They end up relegating the potential opportunity to the back burner and then set off again in search of easier, low-hanging fruit.

Rainmakers don't regard this as a lost opportunity and know that it's actually a great place to apply the Second Place Strategy. When meeting with the customer in this type of situation, here's an example of how you might effectively position the Second Place Strategy.

"Mr. Customer, I appreciate the fact that you have a relationship with company XYZ. At our company, we work hard to cultivate those same types of relationships with our customers. From time to time, however, conditions change and I know no one likes to be left in the lurch without a back-up position. With your permission, I would like to position myself and my company to be your back-up provider. Here's what I mean by that. We'll do our homework on your business. We'll work to understand your issues and we'll bring you information from time to time that we think might be of value to you. And in the event that your first place provider doesn't meet or exceed your expectations, we'll be ready to step up to bat when needed. I've found that most customers agree that this makes pretty good business sense to them. May we have second spot?"

Let's look for a moment at what's happening here. When you first go to see the customer, the perceived value of what you're bringing to the table is low, and that makes the price of change high. Your customer already has a primary provider and there are probably quite a few other vendors all vying for the same business. By asking for and positioning yourself in second place, you essentially freeze any other competitors out of the process.

After you confirm your second place position, it's time to start providing knowledge-based value to this prospective client. On every subsequent contact over the next three or four months, you offer highly relevant, customer-centric information that makes your prospect's life easier. Now ask yourself this, "Is the number one provider doing any of this?" It's highly unlikely they are. One thing is certain, in today's competitive marketplace, it's not uncommon for sales professionals to take their existing clients for granted and this strategy will help you take advantage of that. Once you get second place, you automatically get closer to potential customers and now have an ongoing opportunity to outshine the incumbent. Over the next few months, by treating them as if they were equal to your best customers, you'll be demonstrating the higher level of value you provide which makes the price of change seem much lower. You'll cause erosion of the existing relationship and it's often only a matter of time before you become the preferred provider.

While winning the business right off the bat is great, sometimes being in second spot can be an even better long-term strategy if you're aware of the Value/Price Relationship.

What's Next

Coming up in our next chapter, we take our discussion of value to the next level. I'll show you how you can effectively identify your value at a number of different levels and then how to position it so that it has the greatest impact. When you know how to accurately identify, position and then sell your value, you'll be elevating your sales presentations way beyond the level of mediocrity your customers are accustomed to.

CHAPTER 4

Value-Added Positioning

In this chapter, we're going to look at how you can deliberately and systematically increase the perception of total value to your customers. When you have a solid understanding of how to position your product or service from a value-added perspective, you'll be much better equipped to offset competitive pressure and be far less influenced by market demand to reduce your pricing. If you give in to unjustified pricing pressure, you end up serving no one; not yourself or the customer and it becomes a race to the bottom.

The key to long-term success is to adopt the philosophy of value-added selling as a way to educate your customer base in order to help them make better purchasing decisions and to increase your own profitability. When you position your products or services from a value-added perspective, not only are you employing a mutually beneficial win-win strategy, you're also effectively positioning yourself as more knowledgeable and professional than your competition.

Value-Added Positioning

Value-added positioning is both strategic and tactical. It's strategic in the sense that it should be an integral part of your sales process. It's tactical in how and when it should be applied.

The overall goal of value-added positioning is to differentiate your company from your competition. If you're not able to clearly demonstrate the value-added component of your offering – something tangible that sets you apart – your product or service will be relegated to *same as all the rest* status in the mind of the customer. And as soon as you get slotted into that crowded category, closing the sale becomes much more difficult without having to give in to downward pricing pressure.

If you become focused on value-added positioning, you'll already be standing out from the crowd. Research shows that the majority of sales professionals use price as their sole competitive weapon. They resort to low-ball pricing in order to get the sale. It's bad for them, but good for you if you're a value-added professional.

Interestingly, the latest research also suggests that today's sophisticated buyer will, in many cases, pay a 10-15% premium for a better solution. The same buyer will also pay a 5-10% premium for better service. The key words here are premium and better. Paying a premium means higher profitability for your company and bigger bonuses and commissions for you. The concept of *better* is very subjective – better is whatever the customer perceives as being better. Remember, it's about differentiating your value-added components in the mind of the customer in a way that is relevant to them. If you're doing this effectively and your competition isn't, then you're going to win.

When you become effective at positioning your additional value to customers, your product or service loses commodity status and you set yourself apart from the competition.

Customers are not always trying to get the lowest price for a product or service, but they are concerned with getting the best value. Value-added positioning works by meeting the needs of both parties. This means maximizing the profits of the selling company while providing the best overall value solution to the end user. The key to value-added positioning is that any benefit must be seen as worthwhile and applicable to your customers' needs. If customers don't see a benefit that applies specifically to them, then they'll dismiss it.

The Value-Added Formula

When positioning your product or service's value in the mind of the customer, it's essential that you fully explain the concept of value. It's not just about the price of the product. Price is only one variable and by itself, it is not an accurate representation of true value. The formula for determining the true customer value is:

Price + Cost + Impact = True Value

In this equation, *Price* refers to the acquisition cost. In other words, the actual purchase price of the product or service. This is the amount that the customer writes the check for.

Cost represents the extra, unavoidable costs associated with ownership. This is best explained with a simple example. Let's say that you were purchasing a vehicle and the price tag was $30,000. The sticker price doesn't reflect any of the additional costs or expenses that will be incurred to maintain the vehicle over years of ownership. Examples of these costs might be financing charges, maintenance, repairs and fuel. Over the lifetime of ownership, these costs can vary dramatically from vehicle to vehicle and can really add up.

The *Impact* portion of our equation often refers to something quite apart from the fiscal aspects of a purchasing decision. Going back to our example, let's say that you were trying to decide between a conventionally powered car and a hybrid version. The initial sticker price of the hybrid might be higher, but the lifetime costs might be lower based on lower consumption. But even if they were essentially the same, the impact of your purchasing decision might be quite different. The impact of your decision in this case, beyond the financial considerations, is that with the hybrid, you would be lessening your impact on the environment as the hybrid generates fewer fossil fuel emissions. And that's value of a completely different sort, but of no less importance to many consumers. In fact, to many, it might be *the* deciding factor.

When determining *Cost* and *Impact*, make sure you fully understand how your product or service may extend the life of a customer's product, increase productivity or improve efficiency and make sure you're able to quantify those values.

When all three components – *Price*, *Cost* and *Impact* – are added up, the sum is the *True Value* of your product or service. To be able to take advantage of the power of value-added positioning, salespeople can't just be good at selling; they have to be good businesspeople as well. They must have a broad understanding of how their customer's business works and what impact their own products or services have on their client's business. They need to start from a 30,000 foot perspective to see the bigger picture and long-term implications and then be able to break their offering down into bite size pieces that will logically build upon one another to create a *True Value* solution.

The 3 Levels of Value

Most salespeople today tend to focus their value-added offerings in only one area – that of the product or service. Companies that only employ the product aspect of value, fail to fully maximize their potential with the prospect or customer. The product component of value-added only represents a third of the total value that the customer receives. It's critical that you move beyond this first stage and learn to categorize your value-added components into three individual areas.

You'll see that this will give you a much greater chance of keying in on an area that is of specific interest to each unique client situation. We'll cover each level briefly here as an introduction and then return to them later in the chapter for more specific examples of how to create greater leverage for yourself.

Product Value-Added

As we've already discussed, the first of these separate areas is product. When asked to describe their value-added components, most salespeople will focus in this area. And it's a great starting point. A professional salesperson should always be prepared to provide details as to how their product or service stands out from the competition. But the key is to not stop here. After you have fully described your value added components in terms of your product or service, it's time to add to it by moving on to the next aspect of differentiation.

Company Value-Added

The next area of value-added you need to capitalize on is the company itself. Your company can offer significant value to your product or service if you can highlight the positive differences the customer receives as a result of dealing with your company. When other areas appear to be equal, customers will often choose to deal with companies they see as industry leaders. When there isn't an overwhelming reason, customers don't like the risk involved with taking a chance on an unproven supplier. A positive company track record of providing industry recognized solutions is a valuable asset in your sales toolkit. The reputation your company enjoys is a great leverage point.

Individual Value-Added

The third level of value that you can build upon is that of the individual. That's you! Survey after survey demonstrates that at least a third of the total value the customer receives comes from the salespeople themselves. In other words, salespeople can often make or break the deal. Your experience, knowledge, personal communication style and a dedication to world-class service are often just what's needed to effectively seal the deal. So never sell yourself short – you're a big part of the value-added equation and don't hesitate to ensure your customers know exactly what you can bring to the table for them. And never forget the importance of the likeability factor. If they don't like you, they may overlook any of the other value you offer and they won't buy from you. That's why the same product from the same company offered from two separate salespeople can produce such diverse results. In fact, a customer may even see them as two completely different solutions.

By fully leveraging all three levels of value, you position your product or service as unique and distinctive and can remove it from commodity comparisons. There are no commodities in the world of value- added.

Becoming a Value-Added Specialist

The difference between a specialist and generalist is significant, at least in terms of income and revenue. Specialists, in almost all cases, make more money than those who are generalists. And given a choice, customers would almost always prefer to deal with a specialist. That's just the way it is. Value-added specialists are more successful because they know how to identify all three levels of value and position that value effectively with their clients. They don't take orders, they make orders. And they do it by creating such a high-value solution, that price becomes a less important factor.

To this point, we've learned about the three levels of value-added that you can employ to differentiate your product or service. Now we'll delve a bit deeper and look at how a great value-added strategy can utilize both *quantitative* and *qualitative* elements.

Quantitative elements are things that are tangible, observable and measureable and they tend to appeal to the logical side of our brain in the purchasing decision process. Qualitative elements are more subjective. They're not as easy to measure and tend to be less tangible, but they're equally important, if not more so, because they appeal to our emotional side. And as we know, emotion plays a major role in rationalizing any purchasing decision. Qualitative elements are more

about making the customer feel good about you, your company and
your solution.

Here are a few *quantitative* examples...

Your Company's Profitability. Profitable companies are seen as
leaders and innovators. The bigger and more complex your solution
is, the bigger the benefit to the customer. They see your strong profitability as proof that your solutions have worked in the past and they
can trust your experience.

 Years in Business. Company history goes a long way with today's
customer. A long and strong track record helps to build trust.

Industry Leadership. If your company is established as the industry
leader, that's a real tangible bonus in your favor. Customers like to
associate with winners.

Number of Locations. This could be an important factor when it
comes to just-in-time distribution, or when reach becomes a factor.

Available Resources. Companies that have extra resources available within their own organization or through strategic partnerships
create a very tangible benefit to the customer.

Now let's examine a few examples of *qualitative* elements...

Reputation. Again, if trust is the foundation of all relationships, then
reputations are of high importance.

Your Brand. It's a proven fact that the leading brand can command
a premium price in the marketplace.

Goodwill. If your company has a rich tradition of client support,
community involvement and social responsibility, the goodwill generated by these actions can be a real motivating factor for buyers.

Management Style. How your company is managed, and by
whom, can provide a distinct advantage if your customer admires
your approach.

Identifying Value-Added

The first step to becoming a value-added specialist is to identify the value-added elements of your product or service. So, how exactly do you do this? Where do you start? These are common questions and ones that cause many sales professionals to hesitate, procrastinate or never start at all. Well, there's no need to feel overwhelmed. It's not complicated, but it does involve some commitment on your part and a willingness to do a little bit of investigative homework to get the relevant information.

To get things rolling, your first step should be to write down every value-added element that you can think of that might have an impact on your solution to the customer. And to keep you organized and focused, you'll be dividing them into our three levels of value; *Product, Company* and *Individual*. Resist the urge to analyze them at this point, just get them down first.

Product Value

Let's start with the product component. The main questions that need to be answered here are, *"What benefit does my product or service provide?"* and, *"What overall impact does my product or service have on the customer?"*

Here are a number of product-focused examples to get you started.

- Profitability
- Ease of Use
- Serviceability
- Compliance
- Waste Reduction
- Performance
- Convenience
- Quality
- Efficiency
- Safety

- Speed

Your product or service may address these and very likely many others as well. Your goal at this stage is to identify as many as possible.

Company Value

The second component you will focus on is the company itself. Here are a number of specific benefits that could represent significant added value for your customers.

- Product Selection
- Customization
- Ordering Options
- Ease of Doing Business
- Market Leadership
- Field Support
- Customer Support
- Technical Support
- Online Support
- Loyalty Programs
- Distribution Channels
- Facilities
- Hours of Operation
- Community Involvement

Again, this is not an all-inclusive list, but it will get you pointed in the right direction. Your list should include all the value-added elements from a company perspective that go into providing your solution.

Individual Value

The third component is the individual. That's you – the salesperson. You've got a lot to offer and there's no need to be shy about it. At the end of the day, it's often the relationship between the customer and sales representative that tips the scales in one direction or another. So maximize your leverage by making sure your customer knows just how much you bring to the table.

Here are some individual value-added components to get you started:

- Knowledge
- Attitude
- Passion
- Helpfulness
- Presentations
- Field Support
- Reputation
- Personal Organization
- Appearance
- Sincerity
- Professional Achievements

Again, remember that it's often your ability to relate to your customer that will win the day. You don't need to go overboard, but you do need to make sure that your customers know that their interests are going to be well served by dealing with you.

Quantifying

Once you have identified your value-added components, the next step of the model is to quantify them. That means putting a price to them, at least the quantitative ones. I will often ask salespeople how much their company spends on this or that particular value as I move down their list and, in most cases, they have no real idea. Remember, it's these values that separate you from the competition; they're a primary component of your distinctive value and they play a major role in your differentiation strategy. And yet, most salespeople can't pinpoint their actual monetary value or their impact on the customer. This isn't acceptable for a value-added specialist. You need to know what each of these values is worth.

Once you have identified your value-added elements, take them to your manager and the accounting department and see if you can quantify each of them. It will usually involve breaking down the total cost and separating out the individual value-added elements. You may have to look up a specific line item from the financials. Sometimes you'll have to be a little creative, but whatever you have to do, try to come up a with an accurate cost for each of your quantitative, value-added components. If you can't come up with an exact number, make a best guess based on the information you have. If an actual number value doesn't make sense, perhaps you can come up with a percentage of the total solution cost – anything that establishes the tangible dollar value of these value-added components in the mind of the customer.

Selling Value-Added

The final step in the value-added model is to actively sell the value-added elements. This is why the quantification part of the process is so critical. If you can't put a value to something, how can you sell it? Imagine having a number of products to sell and you have no idea what price to sell them for. And if you can't sell the value, you lose the value – at least in the mind of the customer. We can sell our value-adds on at least three fronts:

1. Annual Work Reviews

Annual Work Reviews are a great way to establish your value-added services and anchor them in the mind of your customer. Let's say for example that your value-added services amount to about 20% of the total value that your customer receives. Here's an example of how you might position this information with your customer...

Salesperson: "Mr. Customer, thank you for setting up this time for our annual review. This is where we like to sit down with you, review our activities over the last year and look for new ways to add value in the upcoming year.

I wanted to show you your purchasing activity for the past year. You've purchased $100,000 worth of our products. You're one of our *best customers and we really appreciate your business.*

I also wanted to show you the value of the services we provided for you that we didn't charge you for. As you can see by this valuation, they represent a total of $20,000. That amounts to a 20% bonus in value. We've been delighted to provide it to you this past year and we'll be happy to provide it again at no charge in the coming year. I just wanted you to know."

In most cases you will get the following response from your customer.

Customer: *"That's very interesting. I had no idea."*

Salesperson: *"Well, Mr. Customer, you're not alone. In fact, most of my customers don't realize the actual value of these services. As I said before, we're delighted to provide the additional value because we truly appreciate our relationship. I just find that most customers are very interested in knowing the actual cost of the extras and welcome the information."*

2. Negotiations

Once you have quantified your value-added elements, you can then use them in your negotiations with a customer. Think of the last time that you purchased an automobile. If you'd been really observant and paid careful attention to the price sheet that is usually attached to the window, you would have seen a quantified breakdown of all the features and options. At the bottom is the sticker price which effectively shows you the sum of all the listed prices. They show you how they came up with the bottom-line number. When it comes time to negotiate the final purchase price, the customer can see the exact value of each component. This makes it easier for the salesperson to customize a solution by removing options if necessary and, at the very least, clearly showing how much actual value the customer is receiving if a component is to be included at no charge.

The value-added strategy is particularly useful when combined with our 3-Solution strategy which I'll be sharing with you in the upcoming *Sales Process* chapter. Each of your three solutions can contain a number of these value-added services and your pricing can reflect the number of value-added elements that are included. Your customer may want to negotiate with you, but at least you're starting the negotiating process from a properly framed position where both parties can clearly see the value of any concessions.

3. Competitive Situations

As a sales professional, you will often find yourself competing against an incumbent vendor or you'll have someone trying to take business away from you. This is where value-added positioning is so effective.

The most compelling reason for effectively positioning value-added services is so that you can isolate and highlight the definable and defendable differences between you and the competition. In some cases, your competition may even offer the same values that you do, but if they fail to properly quantify and position the value, they lose the value. They just won't resonate with the customer.

A useful exercise that will help you apply this strategy is to create a Distinctive Value Matrix. Begin by listing all three levels of value-added elements. Then show how you compare in these areas with your competition.

Here's how it might look at the Product Level...

Product Attributes	*Our Company*	*Competitor A*	*Competitor B*
Availability	B+	C+	C
Packaging	A	B	C-
Warranty	A	B	B
Acquisition Price	C+	B	A-
Quality	A	C+	D
Operation Cost	B+	C	C
Durability	A	B-	D
Performance	B+	B-	C-
Brand Equity	A	C+	C+
Safety	B+	B	B
User Friendliness	A	C	C-

Here's how it might look at the Company Level...

Company Attributes	*Our Company*	*Competitor A*	*Competitor B*
Ease of Doing Business	B+	C+	C
Reputation	A	C+	C-
Technical Support	A	B	C+
Terms	B	B+	B+
Return Policy	A	B-	D
Inventory Levels	B	C	C-
Service Policy	A	B	C+
Ordering Options	C+	B	C+
Industry Leadership	A	B-	C
Post-Sale Support	B+	C+	C-
Pre-Sale Assistance	A	C+	C+

And finally, at the Individual Level...

Individual Attributes	Our Company	Competitor A	Competitor B
Knowledge	A	C+	C+
Follow-Through	A	B	C-
Understanding of Needs	A	C+	C-
Empathy	A	B+	B+
Accessibility	B+	B	C+
Integrity	A	B	C+
Straightforwardness	B+	C	C-
Accountability	A	B+	B+
Innovative Thinking	B+	C	D
Listening Skills	A	C+	C-
Attitude	A	B	B-
Personal Organization	A	C+	C
Make it Happen!	A+	B-	C-

These matrices may not be applicable in every selling situation, but when they are relevant and you've done your homework, they're very powerful persuaders in the eyes of the customer.

Value-added positioning will allow you to diminish price concerns and build value in the mind of your customer. It will give you quantifiable value to work with that has, in most cases, been left untouched. As you focus on value-added positioning, you'll uncover even more areas of value that will help you differentiate your product or service from the competition. Remember, if you don't clearly identify and sell the value, you will lose the value.

What's Next

By now, you're aware of the different levels of value you can draw upon and you've learned how to analyze your current offerings and identify and position your value to create the most impact. But what about creating *new* value? What's the best way to add to your existing mix and create additional value that's seen by the customer as rare, precious and unique? Well, that's exactly where we're headed in our next chapter. We'll explore what makes value truly distinctive and how it can be created on three specific levels. And finally, I'll share with you some of my very best tactical strategies for building value at the highest level of importance to the customer.

CHAPTER 5

Creating
Distinctive Value

In this chapter, we'll take an in-depth look at what it takes to create the kind of value that will make you stand out from your competition. Most companies are quite good at providing value to the marketplace, but they rarely take it any further than that. In today's competitive marketplace, it's not enough to simply provide value. For real success, organizations and individuals must be able to provide *Distinctive Value*.

We'll define it, show you how to create it, how to position it and finally, how to implement it in ways that will separate you from the competition in both the minds and the hearts of the marketplace.

A Definition

The key difference between the average company's definition of value and the Rainmaker version is the concept of distinctiveness. Rainmakers understand that every company must bring value to the market just to be able to compete. Value is the price of admission. But just being in the game is not enough; if you want to win, then you must provide distinctive value.

So what exactly do we mean by distinctive? I define distinctive as something that is not just different, but something that is rare, precious or unique. It's instantly recognizable and the benefit to the end user is clear. And here's the important part – it's not being offered by the competition and it's not typically expected by the consumer. Being distinctive is about separating your company and yourself from the average and the expected. It's about surprising and delighting your customers and potential customers with value that is both memorable and worthwhile. Creating and delivering distinctive value is what will truly differentiate you from the rest of the pack.

Types of Distinctive Value

Providing distinctive value to your customers can be achieved in a number of ways. It's important to be aware of the different types of distinctive value, or DV. This way you can make the best investment of your time and resources. Generally, there are three categories of distinctive value.

Product-Based Distinctive Value

The first type is product-based distinctive value. Many of today's leading corporations can attribute their longevity to product-based DV.

Their success is based almost entirely on the strength of their products. They tend to be innovators and are constantly refining their products with evolutionary and sometimes revolutionary processes. Let's take a look at some examples of the companies that employ product-based DV to create competitive advantage.

Operating Systems

Apple has always been a pioneer in the personal computer industry. Apple created the user-friendly graphic interface that opened up computing to the masses by making standard operating processes simpler and easier to understand. As a result of the ground breaking distinctive value created by the Apple interface, its main competitor, Microsoft, responded by creating their own version of the user-friendly interface – Windows. The old, cumbersome Microsoft DOS interface was rendered obsolete by Windows and, while they weren't the creator of the graphic interface, Microsoft made a strategically historic distribution decision by allowing any PC manufacturer to pre-install Windows on their machines for free. The subsequent market penetration for Windows was massive with Microsoft Windows now being the software used by close to 90% of the operating system market. Even though Apple maintains a zealous and committed base of users, their product-based distinctive value alone didn't create the kind of mass market penetration they had envisioned. They learned their lesson on this one when they introduced iTunes which was made available on both operating systems.

Browser Battles

Netscape changed the world with the invention of the internet browser, but failed to stay ahead of the crowd and lost its leadership position within just a few short years to its originally less innovative competitors. As of January 2015, according to the website StatCounter, 46% of consumers use Google Chrome to access the internet, 21% use Microsoft Internet Explorer, 17% use Firefox, 11% use Safari and the balance is made up of smaller players – no sign of Netscape anywhere in sight!

Companies that live by product-based DV alone, can also die by product-based DV. Unless you are constantly focused on continuous improvement, your innovative technology can go by the wayside. You just can't stand still.

Video Formats

Another classic story that illustrates the potential pitfalls of focusing on product-based DV alone is the Beta/VHS format competition in the early days of video recorder technology.

Both technologies were developed by Sony. However, Sony knew that Beta was, technologically, the superior format. They opted to keep the Beta technology for themselves while allowing the VHS technology to be cross-licensed to other manufacturers. All of Sony's market-ing muscle was put behind the technologically superior Beta format. It was the better product and Sony was confident this would win the day for them. Other manufacturers, out of necessity, adopted the VHS format and flooded the market with VHS machines at a lower price point backed by equally aggressive marketing. The combined marketing efforts of the larger contingent of VHS manufacturers succeeded in creating consumer confusion regarding format superiority and that, com-bined with a tremendous distribution advantage, eventually lead to VHS technology winning the VCR format battle in the consumer marketplace. Beta still enjoyed great adoption in the professional marketplace, but in the battle for the huge consumer market, better technology alone was not enough to win the day.

There are 4 P's in the marketing mix: Product, Price, Place and Pro-motion. Even though Product is an integral part of the mix, a great product by itself doesn't guarantee success. In the case of the VCR format battle, a significant distribution advantage (the Place component), effective marketing (the Promotion component) and a more attractive Price point were enough to overcome the Product superiority of the Beta format in the consumer's mind.

In our Beta/VHS scenario, Sony failed to outdo their competition in 3 of the 4 marketing P's. But it often takes just one slip-up on any of the 4 P's to cause an otherwise great product to underperform. On many occasions, a superior product will fail to catch on due simply to an inferior promotional strategy. If your marketing story doesn't resonate with your audience, you'll face an uphill battle.

What's In a Name?

Such was the case with the Chinese gooseberry, a very tasty little fruit native to the south of China. Struggling to gain acceptance under its original name, exporters in the 1950s briefly renamed it the *melonette* which didn't fare any better. The fruit is now grown mainly in China, Italy and New Zealand and enjoys great success as a result of a bright New Zealand exporter named Jack Turner deciding that calling it *Kiwi Fruit* might just ring a bell with consumers. And the rest, as they say, is history.

Another challenge that becomes inevitable when you have a great product is the window of opportunity for exclusivity. You can bet that the competition won't stand still when they see that you have a competitive advantage in product and sooner rather than later, they'll be introducing a *me-too* version. Let's look at an example...

Short-Lived Exclusivity

In 1994, FedEx added an online package tracking component to their desktop-based PowerShip software. This was a real boon to consumers who could now follow their packages in transit without having to call in to FedEx – a great example of a win-win in product innovation. Greater convenience for the customer and fewer support issues for FedEx. Their distinctive advantage was short-lived, however. Their main competitor, UPS, introduced their own online tracking system in 1995 and what was once distinctive value for FedEx had become just regular value in just one year because someone else now offered the same service.

The takeaway from this story is clear; even if you invent a ground-breaking product or service, it will only give you a competitive advantage for a limited time. If a company relies solely on the strength of its products to secure its position in the marketplace, it will always be looking over its shoulder. Eventually an existing or brand new competitor will create something that is quicker, better, and faster than the incumbent. Remember, what is distinctive value today will only be expected value tomorrow.

Product-based DV is very valuable, but it's important to understand that it's often very expensive and is a never-ending cycle. Innovators must constantly look to the future, re-group when the competition catches up and push the boundaries yet again in order to maintain their image as innovators. This is a daunting challenge for many organizations, but there are examples of innovative companies that do successfully re-group and re-invent themselves.

In October 2001, Apple began a stunning recreation of itself with the launch of the iPod digital music player. The iPod and the imitations that followed have revolutionized the music distribution industry. But the difference for Apple this time around was that they didn't stop with the device itself; their iTunes music distribution system has become the most dominant seller in the retail music industry today with more music sold through iTunes than any other distribution channel.

But unfortunately, the lesson of Apple's remarkable adaptability has not always been learned by other previous market leaders. Here's a classic example of product-based DV erosion.

Hard Lessons

Digital photography has killed many formally big players in the photography industry due to an inability to effectively adapt to change. But there was one company in a position to not only weather the storm of change, but to emerge as a leader. Polaroid was the pioneer of instant photography. If there was ever a company perfectly positioned to lead the entry into the digital photography era, it was Polaroid. Its whole value proposition was centered upon providing images almost instantly. They owned that position in the consumers' minds.

But Polaroid was so focused on its existing product that it failed to see the bigger picture and anticipate where the market was inevitably heading. It abandoned its innovator's market view and has subsequently degenerated to a bit player relegated to the fringes of a market that it was once perfectly positioned to dominate from the consumer's point of view.

Having a strong product is a must in a competitive marketplace. It's the first building block for success, but I hope you can now see that, on its own, it's not always enough. Creating product-based DV is an ongoing process and the expense involved in maintaining a leadership position can be challenging for many organizations.

Service-Based Distinctive Value

When I use the term *service*, I want you to think of it as comprising all components of the total customer experience with the exception of product. Service, defined for our purposes, is everything you do for the customer. It wraps up your product to form the total customer experience and helps to create the emotional connection your company has with the customer.

Every company provides service to a certain extent, but a superior total experience makes customers feel confident they've made the right purchasing decision and helps to eliminate any instances of buyer's remorse. If you think of it as product *insurance*, you're on the right track. Service-based DV effectively surrounds a company's core product or service and elevates its perceived value in the mind of the customer. It helps the customer to rationalize paying a premium for something that might otherwise be essentially the same as the competition's offering.

Elevating a Standard Service

Let me take a moment and illustrate how you can use service-based DV to differentiate a standard product offering. Let's suppose that your car is in need of repair. You take it down to the local repair shop and you'll probably hear something like this...

"Mr. Smith, we need your car for about three hours and it will cost about $150 to repair your vehicle. You're welcome to wait in our service lounge and have a coffee and a muffin while we work on your car, or if that's not convenient, we'd be happy to give you a ride to work and pick you up when it's done."

Now if this sounds familiar, it's because it's so commonplace today.

You can find this level of service just about anywhere. It has become expected by the consumer and has therefore become a commodity. Remember, expected value is just the price of entry into the marketplace. It's not distinctive.

But times are changing and a new auto repair shop comes to town – ABC Auto Body & Repair. When you call them about the same type of service, here's what they have to offer...

"Mr. Smith, we'd be delighted to help you. At ABC, we recognize that not having your car available while it's being serviced can be a real inconvenience, so we offer an option that is geared to help alleviate that stress for you. With your permission, we'll send someone to your home this evening to pick up your car. Our world-class mechanics will work on your car throughout the evening and we'll have it back in your driveway with keys and paperwork in the mailbox by 6:00 a.m. There is a $25 premium in addition to our base price of $150 for this service, but we're finding that many of our customers are taking advantage of this option for the convenience it offers."

So what about you, would you pay the premium? Not everyone will, but many would and some people would gladly pay even a greater premium. For them, the small increase in price significantly outweighs the inconvenience of being without their vehicle. ABC Auto Body & Repair was able to take a standard commodity purchase and elevate it with service-based DV to a point where a substantial portion of the marketplace would be willing to pay a premium of more than 15%.

Extracting a Premium for Service

If you take a look at some of the top service companies in the marketplace, companies like Nordstrom, Four Seasons, Starbucks and Disney, you'll see companies that are able to extract a premium because of the level of service they provide. Service leadership does not come by accident to these category leaders; it's a deliberately chosen, strategic platform that defines the very nature of their businesses. They have recognized that, for them, the way to differentiate their otherwise commoditized offerings in a crowded and highly competitive market-place is to make service leadership an over-riding priority. They've targeted service as the vehicle to drive growth and maintain healthy profit margins. They provide exceptional service and charge a premium for it – a good rule of thumb for any organization. People will pay a premium to feel special.

Service-based DV creates a strong emotional connection with your customers, but only if it's different and unexpected. Too often, com-panies make the mistake of thinking they're providing service-based DV if they're doing a good job of meeting their customers' expecta-tions. Make no mistake, it's essential to meet customer expectations, but meeting expectations alone is not enough to position a company as a service leader and allow it to charge a premium. Again, if it's expected, it's not distinctive. Let's look at a company that truly knows the difference and consistently provides service-based DV.

Keeping it Clean

Disney knows that part of the magic of the Magic Kingdom is ensuring that kids and their parents have a memorable experience that is not im-paired by the operational realities that plague many other entertainment complexes. For example, with the number of visitors that Disney wel-comes on a daily basis, trash accumulation is an on-going operational challenge. Disney knows, however, that the sight of overflowing gar-bage cans on its grounds could seriously detract from its customers' total experience. As a result, you'll never see an overflowing garbage can at Disney or any staff removing garbage in the presence of cus-tomers. Each garbage can is hooked up to The Disney World Vacuum Trash System. The system uses pipes about two feet in diameter that are connected to the bottom of the trash cans to suck all the trash to a central underground collection point where it is then trucked away. No unsightly emptying of trash cans on the surface of the park to negatively impact a visitor's day – out of sight, out of mind. The system is so successful that it's become a model for several other very large buildings in addition to various cities and municipalities.

Disney customers are willing to pay premium ticket prices because they know the experience will be worth it. They know that Disney takes care of all the details so that visitors can relax and focus on enjoying themselves and creating lasting memories. The kind of lasting memories that encourage tremendous word-of-mouth, repeat visits and strong bottom-line results.

More than Just Beans

Starbucks knows that their beverages are just part of the total customer experience. Appealing to all of the senses is part of the Starbucks experience strategy. Take sound for instance. Starbucks appeals to their customers' sense of sound by playing background music that helps to create a comfortable and appealing setting for meeting and connecting with friends and acquaintances. It became so appealing that customers began to ask if they could purchase the songs and it was from those beginnings that Starbucks Entertainment emerged with a wide variety of song compilations being offered on the Starbucks CD label for sale to customers. Starbucks knows that its customers are loyal for reasons not just limited to their coffee and they're constantly looking at ways to enhance their product offering with a service experience that is better than the competition's. And the last time I looked, Starbucks wasn't the cheapest cup of joe on the block.

Total Team Effort

If a company chooses to differentiate itself exclusively on service, then it requires a conscientious effort by everyone in the organization to make every touch point a memorable one. If the combined, overall experience for the customer has weak spots, customers have a tendency to remember the weak areas and forget the rest, especially if the weak areas are glaring. You have to have the total game to be a service-based DV leader, but the results are worth it.

Service-based DV can also provide a good buffer against the speed of change and innovation that can impact product offerings. It can offer a degree of insulation against downward pricing pressure and product obsolescence, based upon the strong loyalty and good will it generates. This certainly doesn't mean that you can ignore your product, but strong service-based DV can afford companies a bit more time to adjust, adapt or catch up without losing too much ground.

Companies that provide service-based distinctive value often create exceptionally loyal customer bases. They insulate their businesses against the competition by employing an important type of distinctive value that can yield real results. But it's not without its challenges. It can be expensive, difficult to implement and maintain, and can eventually be copied by the competition.

Knowledge-Based Distinctive Value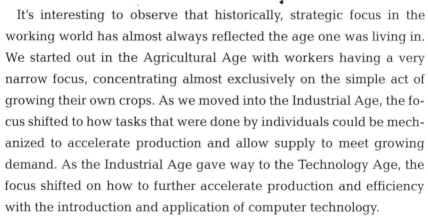

It's interesting to observe that historically, strategic focus in the working world has almost always reflected the age one was living in. We started out in the Agricultural Age with workers having a very narrow focus, concentrating almost exclusively on the simple act of growing their own crops. As we moved into the Industrial Age, the focus shifted to how tasks that were done by individuals could be mechanized to accelerate production and allow supply to meet growing demand. As the Industrial Age gave way to the Technology Age, the focus shifted on how to further accelerate production and efficiency with the introduction and application of computer technology.

Today we have moved into the Information Age. With the flow of information now easier than ever, the most valuable new capital is human once again. But this time it's not physical; it's not brawn, it's brains. Knowledge and ideas are the most valuable commodities in today's business world. Companies that generate ideas and knowledge, companies that manage ideas and knowledge, or those that enable the flow of ideas and knowledge are the ones that enjoy the most success in today's competitive marketplace. Knowledge and ideas are truly the fuel for greatness in the Information Age.

And while most would agree this now is a self-evident truth, few companies are actively focused on creating knowledge and ideas of their own. The day-to-day challenges of managing their businesses often preclude them from devoting the necessary time to this essential element of long-term success. And this is precisely why a knowledge-based DV strategy can be so successful for your company and for you personally.

Why Knowledge-Based DV Works

In Chapter 3, *Value Matters*, we discussed how employing the 5 Customer Currencies can give you greater leverage and increase your sales success. Two of those currencies, the currency of *Time* and the currency of *Knowledge*, are the reasons behind the success of a knowledge-based DV strategy. When we save our customers time by providing relevant knowledge or wisdom that helps them with their day-to-day activities, they're more likely to reciprocate by giving us their business and in many cases, increasing our share of it.

2-Step Process

Creating a knowledge-based DV strategy for your clients is a 2-step process. It's not a one-size-fits-all strategy, but rather a process that needs to be applied to each market niche you work in and often customized to the individual customer within that niche.

Step 1: Identify their Stresses

Every client you work with has his or her own stresses. Often you'll know what some of these stresses might be simply by having a good general knowledge of your customer's industry. Your own under-standing of their business is a good place to start, but if you stop there, you've only just scratched the surface.

Because business relationships, by their very nature, tend to be more formal than personal relationships, most customers will not vol-unteer this key information on their own. If you casually ask a very generic question such as, *"How are things going?"*, customers will try to put their best spin on the answer because they want to be seen as being in control – regardless of whether that's true or not. So the key here is to be more specific with your questions to get the customer to open up and really let you inside their world.

When you meet with prospects or clients, you might try questions like these...

"What kind of business-related stresses are driving you crazy these days?" or...

"What are you finding that gets in the way of maximizing your pro-ductivity?" or...

"What kinds of roadblocks are preventing you or your company from getting where you want to go?"

You'll typically get a wide variety of answers. Responses like...

"We can't find good people."

"The marketplace is really competitive."

"Our competitors are offering deep discounts."

"The economy is eating our lunch."

"We're currently downsizing."

"We're losing good people."

Well, you're probably starting to get the picture. Notice however, that most of their stresses, if not all of them, have nothing to do with you or your product. This is the foundation of the knowledge-based DV strategy! If their stresses have anything to do with your core com-petency, you should already be handling them. But when you address client stresses that are not specifically related to your product or service, you'll be suprising your customers and exceeding their expectations. Customer stresses unrelated to your core competency represent the greatest opportunity for you to differentiate yourself.

Step 2: Providing Knowledge to Address the Stress

Now that you've identified some of your client's stresses, it's time to move on to the next step in the process. You now need to determine what knowledge you can provide or cause to be provided that will makes those stresses go away. Most of the time, the knowledge will have nothing to do with your product or service whatsoever. It should have everything to do with what's stressing out your customer. And that's precisely what will separate you from the pack.

Customers are used to sales representatives providing them with all kinds of information. It's what sales reps like to do. But that information is almost always exclusively related to the product or service the rep's company provides. It may be great information, but it's being provided in order to get the customer to buy something, so it's perceived as really in the best interest of the seller, not the buyer. It may be very valuable in many cases, but the motivation is self-interest and it's expected, so it's not distinctive.

Let's take a look at an example of how a company successfully employed a knowledge-based DV strategy.

Creating a Client University

A client of ours was doing business in a very competitive marketplace. Their main competitor was the market leader who was very aggressive in reacting to any infiltration into what they felt should be their exclusive territory. Our client had great products however – technologically better than the competition's – and they introduced their products to the market with great fanfare and celebration. The marketplace however, failed to see the advantage of their technological superiority and even after two years of significant marketing support, our client had only garnered a couple of percentage points of market share.

So we had them change their focus and tact. Armed with a new-found understanding of the knowledge-based DV strategy, their sales force went into the field and simply asked the target market what their key stress points were. Based on the responses from the market, we went to work with the reps to create the kind of knowledge that would help eliminate the stresses their clients had identified to them. Stresses with their marketing and accounting functions, with their IT and HR departments – whatever was driving them crazy.

Armed with this golden information, we had the sales reps enlist their own marketing, accounting, IT and HR specialists to begin to put together a variety of best practices that would directly address their client's stresses. The sales reps were able to get every depart-ment within their company to provide the necessary intellectual cap-ital to effectively create their own *client university*. This knowledge was then packaged creatively and provided to their customers as a distinctive point of differentiation for their company.

And it worked. During the next two years, they successfully grew their market share from 2% to 55% without any significant change to their product line-up or pricing. And best of all, they were able to con-tinue building market share even when their main competitor reacted by dropping the price of its own product. Because the knowledge they provided was valuable, distinctive and perceived to be in the best interest of the customers and not theirs, the marketplace rewarded them. Knowledge-based DV had generated results that had not been achievable when they were solely focused on product-based DV.

The key is to provide specific knowledge-based information, wherever possible, to help your customers make their own lives easier, to help them do their jobs better or to make them heroes to the people they serve. When you supply knowledge-based distinctive value that either elminates or mitigates customer stresses that have nothing to do with your own offering, you really separate yourself from your competitors that remain focused only on their own products and services. When you partner with knowledge or wisdom, your value once again becomes distinctive.

Endless Opportunity

The best thing about knowledge-based DV is that the possibilities are almost limitless. Because you're not solely focused on your own product, service or industry, the options available to you are really only restricted by your own creativity and ingenuity. You can personalize the knowledge you provide to a company or even to an individual customer within that company. In fact, the more it's customized to the person ultimately responsible for making the purchasing decision, the more effective the knowledge-based DV strategy becomes.

Whatever form your knowledge-based DV ultimately takes, it must all start from the same place. That starting point is identifying the stress and dissatisfaction of your customers. Remember, if they haven't already told you specifically what these stresses are, ask them! If you ask in a sincere and genuine way, people are often more than willing to share their stresses with you. Telling you what's driving them crazy is therapeutic for them. It helps them let off a bit of steam and positions you as a caring listener at the same time. But the difference here is that you're not going to stop at being just a good listener; you're going to use this newfound information to actually help them alleviate these stresses. Hopefully you can make them go away completely, but if not, then at least you'll be able to mitigate their effects. And that positions you completely differently than your competition. It's unique and definitely distinctive.

The knowledge you could provide can take on many shapes and forms depending on the industry and niche you are working within. Over the course of my sales career, I've utilized some very effective types of knowledge-based DV that work well from industry to industry. Let's take a look at some examples.

Technical or Trade-Related Books

With a little investigation, you can often find industry or skill-specific books that are topical and contain information, strategies and techniques that will help your prospects or customers do their jobs better. The subject matter can vary as long as it relates to the customer's role within the organization. For example, perhaps it's the latest book on social media that might be useful to the marketing department, or the latest safety manual for the shipping department. As long as it addresses a stress the company is either experiencing or is anticipating, you're adding value.

Business Books

This one is a personal favorite of mine and I have used it on countless occasions in many different selling environments. This knowledge-based DV strategy is based on the assumption that the prospect or customer has very little time to stay ahead of the curve when it comes to the latest information in the marketplace. When I interview most business executives, their number one stress or complaint is a lack of time to get everything accomplished that they would like.

With this in mind, I routinely dissect the latest business books and search for relevant gems that will provide information useful to the majority of business clients. Often I will highlight key concepts in my own copy of the book and then prepare a brief executive summary, incorporating the selected highlights along with their page numbers. For my really important prospects or customers, I will give them a copy of the book for their own libraries. I try to get a book into their hands several times a year. These prospects often become my customers and I never fail to get a sincere thank you or expression of appreciation.

Book Reviews

In the same vein as the hard copy books that I provide, I also prepare book reviews and regularly send them out to the prospects or customers that I don't provide with copies of books. I include the ISBN number or the link to Amazon.com or their local bookstore in case they would like to order a copy. An important note here – I'm not overly concerned whether or not my prospects or customers actually read the book review. If they do, then so much the better, but what's important is that they see my name in their inboxes with an attachment of value. That's what really matters. It's an important touch point and for a brief moment, customers see my name and know that I was not only thinking about them, but bringing them valuable information related to their stresses rather than my own product or service.

Business Articles

This is another favorite strategy for Rainmakers to build value with their target audiences. When you visit prospects or customers, bring them an article from a popular business magazine that might be relevant to them. Again, this addresses the customer stress of not having enough time to keep up with research. You're saving those customers valuable time by doing the research yourself and providing the information to them. Most current magazines have articles that are topical and wide-reaching, making it relatively easy for you to find something of value. It's easy to provide a link to the article by way of an email or tweet or social media post, but be sure to also bring it up in conversations when you're actually visiting with the customer.

Personal Interest Articles

This is another favorite of mine. I like to assemble articles of specific personal interest that cover many different topic areas. I use the Evernote website and software to store them digitally in file folders devoted to each specific topic and this allows me to easily access them from wherever I am and whenever I want. I also subscribe to a number of popular magazines online and pass along links to the articles I think will best match customer interests. These articles can cover any personal interest that you think might be relevant to certain customers. For example, for customers who love golf, you could compile articles devoted specifically to golf and then use them to create your own *Top 10 Golf Tips* articles, and then send them to your golfing customers every spring before the season starts. Check out allyoucanread.com – it's got a magazine for just about everything.

Speaker Events

Sometimes taking a client out for a meal or to a sporting event is not appropriate and some companies even have policies prohibiting such activities. However, taking a client to a business event where the speaker will be talking about something relevant to the client's business usually passes all scrutiny. A good strategy to help with any policy concerns is to deliver tickets to your customers and let them know you will meet them at the event. Sometimes sponsoring a table and getting your top executive to call their top executive for the invite can also be advantageous.

Interesting Websites

Once you have an understanding of your clients or prospects interests professionally or personally, you can periodically send out links to websites you've visited that may be useful to your customer.

Email Tip of the Week

The email *Tip of the Week* is a strategy we continue to employ with good results. We utilize a sales-related tip, but you might have a technical tip of the week, a safety tip, whatever might be valuable to your clients or prospects. Once you decide on the topic of information, you'll need to determine your level of frequency. For some customers, once a week is appropriate and for others it's once a month or once a quarter. Make sure that when you send the tip, it doesn't include a product ad with the information. Any kind of advertising or marketing content makes the gesture appear self-serving. When the content is pure and relevant, you'll definitely score points with your customer.

Podcasts

There are literally thousands of podcasts from industry experts that cover a variety of topics that you could send your customers a link to. Again, it's not important that they always listen to the podcast; it's important that they see you care about them enough to go out of your way to help them with business issues. If you don't find a podcast that's appropriate, it might be a good idea to create your own. Anyone with a computer and a computer microphone can easily create and post a podcast in today's virtual world. Authoring and producing your own podcast really cements you as an industry expert. And we know that it's predictable human behavior for customers to want to deal with an established expert.

Seminars or Technical Lunch & Learns

Lunch & Learns are always a great way to provide knowledge-based DV to your customer or prospect base. Most people take some time to eat lunch, so if you can combine a learning experience with lunch, particularly if you are paying for it, you can often get an hour of undivided attention and everyone benefits.

Networking Functions

Networking functions are another high-priority activity for Rainmakers. The best application of this strategy is to ensure that any networking event that you create or host provides a direct and tangible benefit and that your guest list includes both customers and prospects. Allowing prospects to mingle with already satisfied customers can be beneficial to everyone. Obviously, you only want to invite customers that are happy with you and your company so that the power of third party endorsements will work in your favor.

The examples I've shared with you represent just a few of the many ways you can provide knowledge-based DV to your customers. I'm sure that you can come up with many others of your own that will help position you as rare and unique in the minds of your customers.

You've no doubt noticed by now that while providing knowledge-based DV is not overly difficult in theory, it does take time to accomplish. That's precisely why it's so valuable! The fact that it takes time to accomplish means that very few, if any, of your competitors, will be employing it. Many salespeople are not willing to put in the effort to create real value for their customers, and even if they are, they're often focused on the wrong things – their own products and services.

Rainmakers know that if they focus on identifying their customers' stresses and can help to eliminate or mitigate them by putting in the work to create knowledge-based DV, they'll position themselves as the emotional favorite in the minds of their customers.

What's Next

So far, we've covered a lot of gound on the subject of value and how you can increase the level of perceived value you and your company provide to the marketplace. Now it's time to start putting it all together in a logical process that can be utilized in virtually any sales situation. In our following chapter, we'll delve into the sales process and why the one you're using right now may not be serving the best interests of your customers. In the new model of selling that you'll learn about, your focus will always be right where it should be – on your customers!

CHAPTER 6

The Sales Process

This chapter will give you some insights about how to construct or modify a sales process that works for your particular business and, when properly executed, will drive new growth. By taking the time to carefully design your process, you can focus your attention on each individual step and be able to determine its impact on your results.

By their nature, sales processes are under constant renovation as products and customers change. Sales professionals that follow a well-thought-out sales process routinely outperform those who don't. In this chapter, we'll work with a simple, yet powerful sales process that will give you an understanding of our approach and serve as a foundational template for your own.

The Traditional Approach

Let's start by taking a look at a typical, traditional approach to selling that is utilized by many sales organizations and salespeople through-out North America. It's used so widely because it actually does produce results. While there are as many different types and variations of sales processes as there are companies, this example of the traditional approach should give you a sense of what we are talking about.

Let's take a closer look at the traditional model of selling in its basic form. Many salespeople spend about...

10% of their time Establishing Rapport
20% of their time Qualifying the Opportunity
30% of their time Describing Features & Benefits
40% of their time Trying to Close the Business

Now it's important not to get caught up in exact percentages – just understand that these figures are generally representative. The key is to pay attention to the flow and the process.

Let's take a moment to discuss the elements. In reality, there are many variations in sales processes and models in the marketplace and it is virtually impossible to cover them all in the scope of this book. Instead, we've simplified these for instructional purposes, realizing there are many nuances that will be unique depending upon the business or segment you're operating in.

Establishing Rapport

Assuming they've called and scheduled an appointment with their prospect or customer, salespeople then spend only about 10% of their face-to-face selling time establishing rapport. They might talk about the pictures on the customers' desks, the awards on their walls; any kind of pleasant small talk to warm them up and get customers to like them. This works well with many buyer styles and is a common practice with sales professionals. It's important to note however, that there are some buying styles where this has a negative effect on the sales call and could cost you business.

Qualifying

Next, comes the qualifying stage. This is where salespeople ask their prospects really great questions about their business, their needs, stresses, challenges, who they currently use and then try to determine if they have good potential as a customer and if so, how large they might be. The questions that might be used at this stage are covered in more depth in the forthcoming *Question Protocol* chapter. Salespeople typically spend about 20% of their time at this stage.

Features and Benefits

From here, the traditional approach, you would move on to describing features and benefits. This is where you demonstrate your product or service and review all of the features and how they will benefit the customer. Salespeople pull out the beautiful brochures that marketing has prepared for them and they begin to tell their product story and why they think it will be a perfect solution for the customer. About 30% of the salesperson's selling time is devoted to describing features and benefits.

Closing

From there, they jump right into the last part of the traditional model – closing. After they've given a world-class presentation or demonstration of their products and services, they then spend a significant amount of their allotted time – up to 40% – trying to close. They try to close by securing a trial, pilot project or demo, or maybe by getting authorization to participate in a request for proposal. They try to close because they see it as the final step in the sales process.

All Too Common

I refer to this as a *traditional* sales model because we see it time and time again across all sectors and within most companies. While there are variations of this model and percentages may vary slightly, they all follow the same basic steps.

The problem with the typical model of selling is that it's so widely used. Everybody does it. The next salesperson that goes in to meet your prospect will start off exactly the same way. They'll try to establish rapport with some small talk, then they'll spend time qualifying. Then they'll tell the prospect about all the bells and whistles of their product and then they'll try to close on something. If you've ever heard the phrase, *"familiarity breeds contempt"*, you'll understand why many buyers react indifferently to this approach. They've seen it so many times that they know how to defend against it. Unfortunately, sales trainers have been reinforcing this model, or variations of it, for decades.

A New Model

In today's crowded marketplace, we need a new model. A model that is not overused. A model that makes us stand out from the crowd and separates us from the competition. A model that forms the foundation for your overall sales process.

The Underlying Foundation

The model I'll share with you is designed with the underlying premise that trust is the foundation of all relationships. It works in virtually every selling situation if each step in the model is executed properly as described. First, let's take a look at the model and then get into the specifics of each step. Again, don't get hung up on the percentages. It's the flow that matters.

40% of our time is spent Establishing Trust
30% of our time is devoted to Listening
20% of our time is spent on Customizing
10% of our time is spent on Confirming

Establishing Trust

Most people agree that *trust* is the foundation of all relationships. If they don't trust you, they won't buy from you. It's important to note here that trust is earned. Establishing trust often takes a considerable amount of time and is achieved much more easily when you spend a greater amount of time asking questions that will help you find common ground with the customer. When you find something that you can both relate to, then you begin to be viewed as more of a contemporary or colleague and not just a salesperson. The level of trust between you and the customer begins to elevate. Creating trust is such an important issue that our new model suggests that you spend up to 40% of your available time building a trust bond. It really is that important.

Listening

The next step in our model is *listening*. If we're listening, then our customer or prospect is doing the talking. When the customer is talking, you become the trusted advisor. When you're talking, you're just a salesperson. To become a trusted advisor, you need to be asking some really good questions; questions that get the customer to open up and provide you with valuable information. Remember, you have two ears and one mouth and that's the ratio in which you should be using them. Listen twice as much as you speak. Don't try to remember all of the questions you should ask – you just can't. Instead, in your pre-meeting preparation, try to anticipate all of the primary questions you would like to ask and put them down on paper so you have them ready for your meeting. Asking questions and listening is all part of building trust. We should be devoting at least 30% of our available time to listening.

You can see with our new model so far that with 40% of our time spent establishing trust and another 30% spent listening, a total of 70% of our total time is spent on customer-focused activities.

Customizing

The next step in the model is *customizing*. I can't really help you on this one. This is based entirely on your knowledge of your products and services, your experience in the industry and your years on the planet. It's the culmination of all of your business and personal experience. This step will be different from one sales professional to another. And it's really more art than science. Your experience combined with your intuition will allow you to adapt to the given situation. Take what you hear and combine it with what you know to customize. But make sure you do it in that order – in other words, listen carefully first before you start using your experience to customize. Customizing your solutions will solidify your expertise and reinforce to your clients that your goal is to provide specific solutions to their unique needs. In our new model, you'll devote up to 20% of your time customizing your solutions.

Confirming

Finally, we have the *confirming* part of the model. This is significantly different than the closing step that we have seen in the traditional model. The traditional model utilizes closing techniques because typically, not enough background work has been devoted to building a make-sense solution that answers all the customer's needs. And this is why closing can be so difficult and in many instances ineffective. When you're trying to land the business quickly, it often boils down to a moment in time where customers are either in or they're out. They give you a yes or no decision. Yes, you get the business or no, you don't. Even if the solution is the best available, customers often say no because they're just not convinced yet that their needs are being put above those of the salesperson. Experienced buyers can spot closing techniques a mile away and they're very good at deflecting them.

So how do you confirm the business? What's the difference between closing and confirming? How can you get the customer to see the value in your solution so that the *yes* decision is the most logical next step? And how can you accomplish this without having to resort to out-dated closing techniques? To make the new model come to life so that we can confirm business rather than close it, we need to examine the individual steps that fit within our new selling model.

7 Steps to Sales Success

Okay, so I've introduced you to a new model of selling; one that devotes more time to building trust and developing make-sense solutions instead of the traditional model of selling that so many companies still utilize. But to get to the final stage in our new model, which involves confirming the business rather than closing it, we need to carefully examine a sequential series of steps; steps that will make confirming the business seem like the most logical thing to do.

The 7-step process we'll examine here has been used effectively time and time again. In fact, you may already be employing some of these steps in your current process. Here are the 7 sequential steps involved:

1. *Identifying Prospects*
2. *Gaining Access*
3. *Briefing*
4. *Analyzing Needs*
5. *Presenting Solutions*
6. *Negotiating*
7. *Confirming the Business*

1. Identifying Prospects

The first step in any sales process is identifying prospects. Who in the marketplace has the potential to be converted into a customer? It's always a challenge for sales organizations to fully qualify their potential customers and a lot of time and effort goes into creating qualification criteria. At this stage of the process development, it's important to create your criteria from two distinct perspectives – the customer's and yours.

From your company's perspective, you need to determine the most important end goal. Is it growth potential? Market profile? Cost to service the account? Segmentation and alignment? There could be many objectives here from the seller's viewpoint.

Now it's time to look at it from your customer's perspective. What's in it for the prospect or customer? What need does the product or service fulfill? How strong is our value proposition? How do our products and services align with their business? What impact does it have on their business or individuals within their business?

You'll also need to understand how your relationship with the customer is aligned. Who initiated the contact? Which segment or niche do they belong in? What is the quality of our business information? Is there a Request for Proposal (RFP) on the table? Who are the decision makers? What other relationships are we competing with? Who are the gatekeepers?

By applying these qualification standards to your prospect database, you'll save yourself hours of time, which will allow you to focus your efforts on legitimate opportunities. When you take the time to fully assess each opportunity based upon effective qualification criteria, you'll be able to prioritize your opportunities and have a better than average chance of success.

2. Gaining Access

Once we've identified and qualified our prospects, the next step is to gain access to them. There are a number of strategies that companies employ to gain access and get the first meeting. I'll share with you a very professional approach that works well in a variety of situations. You can modify it to fit your own business, but make sure you include some of the key words and phrases that we demonstrate here.

Gaining access often begins with a phone call. When calling new prospects, it's important to remember that you're calling people that you have no relationship with and then expecting them to set aside their precious time to listen to a list of all the features and benefits of your product or service. In most instances, you can expect a natural resistance to your call. Your job is to first build a foundation of trust and then pique their interest as soon as possible.

Here's a sample dialogue for an outgoing call:

"Hello, Mr. Jones, this is Michael Vickers with XYZ Company. Thanks for taking my call. How are you today?"

"Fine, what can I do for you?"

"Mr. Jones, I understand you are the person responsible for manufacturing processes at ABC, is that accurate?"

"That's correct." (if he's not, he can refer you to the person responsible)

"I'm not sure we have anything to be talking about Mr. Jones, that's why I'm calling. One of my roles at XYZ Company is to brief operations managers on some of the new technologies we have developed and how they improve the manufacturing processes, reduce costs and create a better solution for the end user.

"Again, I'm not sure we have anything we should be discussing, but with your permission, in the next couple of weeks, I'd like to schedule a 20-minute briefing with you to meet you personally, show you how we have helped other companies in your industry improve their processes and reduce costs and then determine if there is anything we need to be discussing."

Anatomy of the Call

Now let's take a look at the anatomy of this call. I know it's a simple example, but there are a number of elements that are worth investigating a bit further.

First of all, I'm operating under the basic assumption that the customer has no interest in my phone call and I've even stated it. *"I'm not sure we have anything to be talking about."* How could we? We haven't even met yet. Right away my call is different because customers are used to salespeople calling and immediately claiming that their products will be perfect for the customer's needs. I didn't make that assumption in my call.

Next, I moved on to the reason for my call. Notice that I used the word *brief* in my next statement. *"One of my roles at XYZ is to brief operations managers on some of the new technologies we have developed and how they improve the manufacturing process, reduce costs and add value to the product."*

Briefings are generally information-based and don't scream, *"I'm a salesman and my job is to sell you something!"* I also included at least three benefits in my statement – improve the manufacturing process, reduce costs and add value to the product. I'm hoping at least one of the benefits resonates with my prospect.

Notice I also said *"in the next couple of weeks"*. If you call up a prospect and say, *"Mr. Jones, can I come and see you tomorrow?"*, you're sending a loud and clear message that you're desperate and not very busy. The key with this tactic is to ask for the briefing several weeks out, and the farther out the better. This way, your message implies that you're busy and it will increase your odds of actually scheduling a briefing. Here's how you might position it.

"Mr. Prospect, with your permission in the next couple of weeks I would like to schedule a 20-minute briefing with you." Notice here that I am deferring to him by asking his permission to continue to the next point of contact. By suggesting a 20-minute meeting, the prospect views it as low-commitment with little to lose.

An Alternative

Here's an alternative approach I also find works well to secure your briefing at a farther out date. Let's suppose today's date is May 27th. I call the prospect and say, *"Mr. Jones, I would like to schedule a 20-minute briefing with you for the last week of June."* You're essentially tagging your request with a specific time. Again, this makes the prospect assume that you're extremely busy and that's always a good thing. Another advantage to setting up the briefing so far ahead is that prospects are more likely to actually keep the appointment. If you call them up and schedule an appointment within the next few days, they know they can easily cancel on you and reschedule if necessary. If you call the dentist's office for an appointment and they schedule it weeks in advance, you're more likely to keep the appointment.

Once I have them confirming a date in their appointment book for the last week of June, I'll sometimes offer the following as an alternative, but only if I'm not already booked.

"Actually, Mr. Jones, I'll be in the neighborhood later next week if that is more convenient for you. Otherwise June 24th works perfectly."

Getting back to my original call dialogue, let's take special note of the following section of the call:

"I'd like to schedule a 20-minute briefing with you, to meet you personally, show you how we have helped other companies in your industry improve their processes, reduce costs and then determine if there is anything we need to be discussing."

Notice that I use the word *show* in part of my introduction. I am simply anticipating a possible objection to the meeting such as, *"Why don't you send over the info?"*, or *"Can you email the details?"* By anticipating the objection first, you can be more proactive in your response to any objection. *"As I already mentioned, Mr. Jones, it requires explanation and it would definitely be best to show it to you."* This approach is a strong way to begin your conversations and will enhance your first appointment success ratios. The more you practice and utilize this approach, the better you'll get at it.

3. The Briefing

The briefing is at the very heart of the selling process. It sets the stage for everything else and if it's done well, you can expect more positive outcomes. Within the briefing stage, we employ sales strategies and tactics that are specifically designed to build value in the eyes of the prospect.

Always start your briefing with a confirmation of the time allotted for your meeting. For instance:

"Thank you, Mr. Jones, for taking the time to meet with me. We had originally scheduled for 20 minutes. Does that time frame still work for you?"

The customer will let you know how much time you can spend if you ask them. In many cases, they will actually give you more time if you have established good rapport and piqued their interest. Once your timing has been confirmed, you can begin with the first stages of our new selling model – establishing trust and listening. Earlier in the chapter, we talked about the importance of building rapport and how asking great questions and then listening carefully will position you as a colleague rather than just a salesperson. We will cover in greater detail the type of questions to ask and the proper sequence to ask them in an upcoming chapter.

The key to a great briefing is to ensure that you are gathering customer information rather than distilling your own product or service information.

4. Analyzing

Towards the end of the briefing stage, you may actually have a pretty good idea of what will work for the customer, but be sure to hold off on presenting any kind of solution just yet. What you're doing here is simply gathering all the information you need to take away and thoroughly analyze the customer's needs in order to customize your solution.

Once you've gathered all the information you need, here's how you might position your next step to the customer:

"Thank you, Mr. Jones, for your time. This is what I'd like to suggest at this point. You've been very candid in our conversation and I'd like to take the information you've shared with me today, analyze it a bit more carefully and review it with some of the specialists at my company. That way I can prepare a few courses of action for you to review so that we can find the perfect solution for your needs. Would

that be okay with you? When would be a good time for us to meet for
our debrief?"

Most customers will respect and appreciate the fact that you haven't
tried to sell them anything at this first briefing. Everyone wants a carefully thought-out solution and that's exactly what you've promised them
by asking for the time to carefully analyze their needs. At this point you
can try to set up the timing for your next meeting where you'll be
presenting your solutions.

Remember, your goals at the briefing are to build rapport, listen and
gather information so that you can further analyze it and confirm your
next meeting. You're not providing any answers or solutions at this point.

5. Presenting Solutions

So far, you've met the customer, had your briefing and asked lots of
really good questions. You've gone back to your office, analyzed the
customer's needs and sought out advice from your own people. It's
now time to present your solutions to your customer.

Of course in this example, I'm describing this to you in its simplest
form, understanding that you may have had several calls or visits with
the customer, had your technical people talk to their technical people
and garnered support from others within the organization. This can
be as simple or as complex as the situation calls for; it doesn't matter.
What matters is that you're now prepared to present your solutions or
courses of action.

In the traditional sales model, most sales professionals only present one solution or course of action to their customer. The problem
with this approach is that it usually boils down to a yes or no decision
from the customer. Basically, we make our best guess as to what the
customer may go for and then cross our fingers and hope for the best.
The one thing I can tell you for sure is that when you propose only
one solution or course of action to your prospects or customers and
they say yes right away, you've left money on the table – you just

don't know how much. As a sales professional, I became very frustrated always trying to figure out what the customer would pay for the solution. After all, my job was to maximize the value for my company and the customer's job was to minimize the price they would have to pay. Either way, it required a very educated guess in order to find the perfect solution.

The 3-Solutions Strategy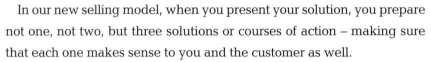

In our new selling model, when you present your solution, you prepare not one, not two, but three solutions or courses of action – making sure that each one makes sense to you and the customer as well.

By preparing three solutions, you gain some flexibility and most importantly, remove the guesswork from the equation.

Solution #1 is the Budget Option

With the budget option, you've removed all the bells and whistles, but still provide a core solution that will do the job. It's important that this is your economy solution. In essence, it's the lowest price that you can provide the service for and still fulfill the customer's requirements.

Solution #2 is the Middle of the Road Option

The middle of the road option is also a perfectly viable solution; it just has a few more bells and whistles. Your job will be to figure out what those options will be. When you know what they should be in a given situation, you add them to your budget option. Don't include everything available, just enough to enhance the offering.

Solution #3 is the Full Meal Deal Option

The full meal deal option is the premium solution. It has all the bells and whistles and is completely loaded. It's your premium offering with the greatest value to both the customer and you.

Here's how you might present your three options to your prospect

The Sales Process   97

or customer:

"Mr. Jones, based on our previous conversations and all the information you've provided to me, I have prepared 3 possible solutions that make sense to me as a specialist at XYZ Company.

"Solution #1 is the budget solution. It will do the job for you, and has been stripped of any additional features or options that are not critical or essential.

"Solution #2 does everything the first solution does, however we have added..." This is up to you to figure out. It could involve delivery, quantity, an upgraded version, etc.

"And Solution #3 is the premium solution. It has all the bells and whistles. It has ..." Again, make sure you add some very tangible extra value here such as improved quality, additional features, etc.

At this point, you've described all the options completely to the customer. Your next step is to confirm the business. Now watch the wording on this part – it's essential you follow this format as closely as possible.

"So, all three solutions or courses of action I've presented will do the job; all three meet your requirements; all three make sense to me as a specialist at XYZ Company. Which one makes most sense to you?"

There's no guessing here. All three solutions or courses of action must make sense. The key is to position the solution you want to sell in the middle, because about 50% of the time, that's the one customers will choose. About 25% of the time they'll pick the budget option and 25% of the time they'll opt for the full meal deal. The actual percentages may vary from transaction to transaction but they'll be pretty close.

What Drives the Budget Choice?

Now what might cause the customer to pick the budget option? You probably guessed it – **price**! Remember, price is never the issue unless it *is* the issue and when it's the issue, *it's the only issue!*

There are some customers who will always choose the budget option, just as there are some customers that will buy the most expensive option. The majority of buyers however, will select the middle of the road option.

The advertising industry spends millions of dollars each year teaching us to buy this way, and it's a strategy that works very well. For instance, if you were buying an automobile, you would have a choice of a stripped-down base model, one with a few extras but nothing too overwhelming and then finally, the top-of-the-line edition with absolutely everything you could possibly think of thrown in. Think of it as good, better and best. If you're ever looking to buy a new iPhone, iPad or iMac, take a look at the options offered on Apple's website. You'll see three different variations for each device, each with varying specifications for memory, speed and options included. I'm sure the more you think about it, the more you'll agree that having more than one solution just makes sense.

Don't Leave Money on the Table

The one variable, however, that you can never be completely sure of as a sales professional is exactly how much a customer is willing to pay. But as I mentioned earlier, one thing you can know for certain is that when you only provide a single solution and the customer says yes right away to the price you've presented, you've just left money on the table! Providing three viable solutions eliminates any guess-work about customer price sensitivity and will ultimately improve your margins and profitability.

Another advantage to providing three solutions is that some customers like to get at least three separate bids or quotes. Their superiors may even require it. When you provide three solutions for consideration, you may very well have eliminated that issue.

Building Trust

Another advantage of the 3-solution strategy is that is has a dramatic impact on the issue of trust. Let me give you an example:

Let's suppose that I repair automobiles and you bring your car in to my service station. I take a look at it, run a few diagnostics and then announce to you that you will need to spend $1500 to repair your car. You then react negatively to the news and explain to me that you have kids in sports, school has just started and... well, you get the picture.

I see that you're now heading out of my repair shop and I'm about to lose a sale. I immediately explain to you that we can always repair some of the work at a later date and bring the quote down to $900. What is our trust level like at this point? If you thought low, I'd agree with you. It's lower because I didn't submit the lower cost option for consideration earlier – instead I just presented the more expensive option.

The second you reduce your pricing, you demonstrate to the customer that your first solution was over-priced to begin with.

Now let's apply our 3-solution strategy to the same situation and see what it could look like.

"Mr. Customer, I have looked at your vehicle and have determined that there are three courses of action we could follow.

"Option #1 would be your least expensive alternative. At the very least we need to repair your brakes. They are well below a safe level and these should be done as soon as possible. This will cost $350.

"Option #2 involves a few more items. If we're going to do the brakes, it would make sense to clean up the rotors as well. This will ensure longer brake life and maximize your stopping power. We noticed your belts are starting to wear out and you have limited life on those. Most likely you will be replacing them in a couple of months anyway. It's far more convenient and cost effective to replace them here than on the side of a highway. The cost for us to do your brakes, rotors and belts would be $600.

"Option #3 involves a more comprehensive solution. During our test drive, we noticed that your transmission is starting to slip. Our

guess is that you have another three months before it starts causing you problems. When transmissions start to go, they tend to go quickly. If you're lucky, you might get a few months longer, but regardless, you're looking at a new one in pretty short order. If we did the work combined with everything else we're doing, we could offer you a significant package discount, and our two year warranty on the work would keep you on the road for years to come. This option is $1500.

"All three options are viable. It's really an issue of your time and budget. Which option makes most sense to you?"

Now here is an important strategy to pay attention to. If you present three options to your prospects or customers and they select your top option 7 out of 10 times, you might want to think about shifting your top option to the middle and designing a new top option. The 3-solution strategy is really your market barometer. On the other hand, if customers buy your budget option 7 out of 10 times, then you're probably on the high side and should adjust the three options accordingly.

6. Negotiating

Negotiating with customers is a fact of life and can be one of the trickiest steps in the sales process. Another advantage of the 3-solution strategy is that you'll find that customers will be less inclined to negotiate because you've already done the work for them by presenting three options at various price points. The very best scenario for you is to assign a specific value to each item or option of a particular solution. By laying out exactly what is involved in each option and the cost associated with it, customers know exactly what they're getting, what they're not and how you came up with the final price of each solution presented. They'll be less inclined to ask for a lesser price if they know that it won't include an option that they really want.

If they still ask for a discount, you can start by asking them which particular item or option they would like to forego. Ask them if they're aiming to get to a particular price point and then show them how by removing specific items, this may be achievable. This won't always solve all your negotiating issues, but it gives you a much stronger starting position and the level of trust will be much higher when everything is laid out in full for the customer to see. Transparency is always your ally in negotiations.

7. Confirming the Business

As you can see, if you've completed all the steps up to this point in our process, there's really no need for time-worn closing techniques. You've covered all your bases. You've gathered good information, analyzed customer needs carefully and then provided a range of solutions that all make sense. You just need to confirm with your customer which one they'd like to go with. Just as with any other process, you still need to ask for the order and be sure you do. It's just that with our new model, you're much more of a trusted advisor than just a salesperson and you've planted the seeds for a much better long-term relationship built on trust.

Additional Guidelines

While adopting and following the steps in our new sales model will lead to greater success, sometimes specific tactics will need to change depending on the situation. You may need to adapt the model slightly to arrive at the best approach for your business. Observing the best salespeople in your organization is a great place to start. What are they focused on? The highest volumes? The highest margins? The most new accounts? Or perhaps it might be about maintaining the existing customer base. Your sales process should be as dynamic as possible and flexible enough to allow you to customize as specific situations dictate. The following guidelines to help you successfully model your sales process:

Create Customer Centered Value

An effective sales process will identify where you can create value. Understanding fully how the process creates value for the customer is essential if you are to generate better results. Customers must be able to easily recognize that any value identified is in their best interest first and foremost if you are to gain their trust and create good long-term relationships. If you fail to create value as the customer defines it, they will ultimately ignore you and buy from your competition.

Prioritize the Objectives

Make sure you know what's most important to your customer and the overall hierarchy of their needs so that you can address them appropriately in your solutions. If your solutions don't address your customers' most pressing concerns, then they're not truly make-sense solutions.

Always Measure

The steps or tasks in your sales process provide data that you can measure and then use for comparison purposes. When you consistently track your activities and generate data that you can measure, you'll provide yourself and your company with essential feedback for further tailoring or adjustment of the process.

Common Vision

The purpose of the sales model is to create a better relationship with your customers by aligning both parties to a common vision. When you align the needs of your customer with those of your organization, you have the basis for mutual respect and strong relationships that are better insulated against the challenges of your competition and a changing marketplace.

What's Next

At the very heart of every sales process lies the essential ingredient that all subsequent success is dependent upon – *questions.* The quality of questions you ask in any given sales situation will determine how well you can build the perfect solution for your customers' needs. The questions you ask not only reveal information, they can also cement your position as an industry expert in the eyes of your customers.

In our next chapter, we'll look at an extensive set of question categories and how you can build a specific question protocol that will ensure you're asking great questions in a thoughtfully sequenced order that will yield better information and ultimately, better results.

CHAPTER 7

The Question Protocol

In this chapter, we'll look at how you can develop and employ a questioning protocol that will help you gain better information, increase your level of trust and ultimately allow you to provide the very best solution for your customers' needs. It's designed to remove the guesswork from the sales process and provide a perfect solution for your customer. You'll learn how to construct and deliver high-value questions that will increase your sales production.

Your Most Powerful Tool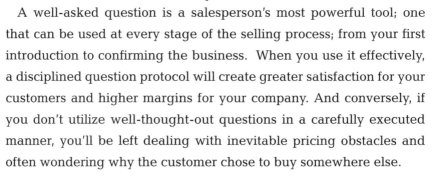

A well-asked question is a salesperson's most powerful tool; one that can be used at every stage of the selling process; from your first introduction to confirming the business. When you use it effectively, a disciplined question protocol will create greater satisfaction for your customers and higher margins for your company. And conversely, if you don't utilize well-thought-out questions in a carefully executed manner, you'll be left dealing with inevitable pricing obstacles and often wondering why the customer chose to buy somewhere else.

This chapter will give you practical insights on how to ask better questions; questions that will help you collect deeper and more detailed information about your customer, ensure that your customers are thinking about what you want them to think about and create a perception of competence and expertise in the customer's mind while building trust and buy-in from your customer.

The Foundation

Well-thought-out questions, in my opinion, are the very foundation of the entire sales process. Your job as a sales professional is to identify your customers' specific needs and provide a solution that is perfect for them. That perfect solution will reveal itself based upon the information you solicit from the customer. Asking a good question gives you the opportunity to get better information; information that will help you and your customer arrive at the perfect solution. It's an old adage, but it really applies here – listen twice as much as you speak. Most salespeople make the mistake of immediately jumping into a product feature presentation and then proceed to discuss all aspects of a particular product – what I like to call a feature dump – without going through the process of fully understanding their customer's needs. Best-selling author, Steven Covey coined a phrase that should become a mantra to be memorized by all prospective sales professionals before they ever enter the sales arena; *"Seek first to understand, then seek to be understood."* So what exactly does *"seek to understand"* mean? It means that before you ever demonstrate or present your product or solution you must first gain a thorough understanding of the customer's needs and that means you are going to have to create and ask some high-value questions.

Establishing Trust

Most would agree that trust is the foundation of all relationships. If the customer doesn't trust you, they won't buy from you, unless of course they don't have any other options. So the question you should be asking is, *"How do I build trust quickly?"* Well-designed questions are the key to creating customer interest, establishing trust and uncovering specific needs. Let's take a look at how you might start off your introduction to a customer with a series of good questions. In the following example, you've just sat down with a prospective customer and are in the process of introducing yourself and your company.

"Thank you for meeting with me, Mr. Customer. I'd asked for twenty minutes. Are we still okay with that time frame? I have prepared a number of questions that will help us stay focused and make the best use of our time today. Would you mind if I ask them?"

By asking the customer for permission, it makes the customer feel as if they're in control and it puts them at ease. Once you've got their go-ahead, you can start to ask your well-thought-out and structured questions.

The purpose of the question protocol is to systematically reveal more and more information about your customers and their needs and requirements. Carefully designed questions will peel back any layers of apprehension and resistance and give you greater access into the customer's mindset.

Focusing on Primary

There are two levels of questions to pose to customers; primary questions and secondary questions. For the purposes of this chapter, we're going to focus on the primary questions. The secondary questions are the ones that follow from the answers provided by your customers to the primary questions. They will come to you naturally as you practice with the primary questions and gain more experience. But before we begin with the actual questions themselves, it's worthwhile to examine a bit of the background theory behind the protocol.

Question Value

There are many different types of questions that you could ask your customer. But not all questions are created equally. Every question has a level of importance or value in the mind of the customer. Your job is to systematically escalate the value of the questions.

Buying Influences

We know that purchasing decisions are based on a combination of logic and emotion. The initial buying impulse is often triggered by an emotional desire. This is followed by the logical step of information gathering prior to purchase. Even though both emotion and logic have come into play in the preliminary stages of the buying process, at the actual time of the purchasing decision, the buyer is often more strongly influenced by the emotional desire and will use logic as a secondary criteria to justify the emotional need. It's important to remember that this is not something a customer will readily admit to – we all would like others to believe that our decisions are driven more strongly by logic than emotion – but the truth is that emotion is often the stronger of the two forces in driving purchasing behavior.

The Value Line

In order to better categorize your questions, it's important to realize that not all questions have equal value to both the buyer and seller. I like to think of the difference in a visual way. I start my categorization exercise by drawing a horizontal line on a piece of paper; a line I call the *Value Line*.

The Value _____
Line

Questions are placed above the Value Line if they have a higher mutual value to both the buyer and the seller.

Some questions will be more inherently logical in nature while others will be more emotionally focused. As we move forward, you'll see that while both logical and emotional questions can exist on either side of the Value Line, in most instances, logical questions reside below the Value Line and emotional questions are situated above the Value Line. This follows naturally from our understanding that emotion is most often the stronger driver of purchasing behavior.

Question Order

The Question Protocol I'll describe for you systematically and chronologically elevates the type of question being asked in terms of value to the customer. We begin first with logical questions which are of lower value to the customer and progressively move up to more emotional questions which are higher in value. Let's explore some of the question categories and review some examples of each.

Status Quo Questions

Status Quo Questions are the first type of questions you should be asking. They are almost always logical in nature and are situated below the value line.

The Value Line _____

Status Quo Questions

They're designed to probe the customer's mindset and discover the current status of the situation. They help us uncover essential facts and establish credibility in the mind of the customer. Examples could include, *"What are you currently using?"*, *"How long have you been using it?"* or *"Are you currently looking for process improvements?"* These are all questions that will give you some insight as to how serious this buyer may be. They uncover key facts that will be important to build upon. While you're uncovering facts, it's important to establish your own credibility. A question that is designed to establish credibility will demonstrate to the customer that you have in-depth knowledge of your subject matter. By being very specific in nature, the question is seen as one that only an experienced professional would ask. For example, *"How familiar are you with XYZ purifica-*

tion technologies?" or, "Would you be interested in hearing how our proprietary manufacturing systems improve performance?" These are examples of industry-specific questions that demonstrate to your customer that you are knowledgeable about your product or service.

Issue Identification Questions

Once we've asked some Status Quo Questions to determine the current environment for this customer, we can move on to *Issue Identification Questions*. While still below the Value Line and logical in nature, Issue Identification Questions start to reveal more valuable information.

The Value
Line
_____

Issue Identification Questions
⬆
Status Quo Questions

Issue Identification Questions are designed to identify any potential issues, challenges or problems that would prevent the customer from moving ahead. Issue Identification Questions facilitate the first stage of problem solving. Again, these are often lower in value to the customer but help you identify the key areas where a solution is required. Some Issue Identification Questions might be, *"How is your current system limiting your growth?"*, *"What reliability challenges does your equipment have now?"* or, *"Is there anything you've seen or heard so far in your research that has caused you any concern?"*

Consequence Questions

Once you've identified any specific issues your customer may be concerned about, you can now begin to move above the Value Line, The next type of question in the protocol and the first type that falls above the Value Line is the *Consequence Question.*

Consequence Questions

The Value
Line

_____

Issue Identification Questions
▲
Status Quo Questions

Consequence Questions are designed to get the customer to think about the consequences of an issue. These questions are very powerful because it is the consequences that will ultimately help customers justify the purchasing decision. *"What would happen if you didn't purchase?"* *"What would happen if things just stayed the same?"* You want to establish the consequences faced or any impending risks. And you want the customer to identify these risks whenever possible. When a customer identifies a consequence or risk, it seems more real – and less of a selling technique by the salesperson. Once you have the consequences of one issue, jump back down below the line and try to identify any other possible issues. Go back and forth; issue to consequence, issue to consequence, back and forth over the Value Line until you've exhausted all the possibilities. For example, *"How does equipment break-down affect your overtime expense?"*, *"How does the complexity of your equipment impact your training or turn-over costs?"* or, *"How will inaction impact your organization?"* These questions really get the customer thinking on an emotional level about how a lack of action may impact their future. You're now starting to ask the questions that have real value to the customer.

Solution Questions

The highest value questions are *Solution Questions.*

Solution Questions
🔺
Consequence Questions

The Value
Line
_____

Issue Identification Questions
🔺
Status Quo Questions

Solution Questions motivate the customer to move forward in the purchasing process by focusing on solving whatever problem they may have or offering benefits or insights in areas of importance or interest. For example, *"What are the essential elements that must be included in our recommendations?"* or, *"Ideally, when do you need these issues solved by?"* These questions will only become apparent when you have gathered enough information to find out the hierarchy of needs for your customer. The greatest value will come from appealing to the highest level of need or desire.

Sequencing is Key

The key is to be asking great questions and asking them in a carefully designed sequence. Think of it in terms of a doctor making a diagnosis. What happens when you meet with your doctor? He or she asks questions and identifies issues before making a diagnosis. A recommendation is never offered before all pertinent questions have been asked and all consequences and risks have been assessed. The recommendation is the final culmination of a disciplined questioning protocol. So if you can start thinking like a doctor, you'll be on your way.

Become a Great Interviewer

Asking well-thought-out questions will help you to accelerate your sales cycle and strengthen the relationship with your customer. They also contribute directly to your customer's satisfaction with you and your company and the level of relationship you enjoy.

To achieve the highest levels of success, every sales professional should strive to become an effective interviewer. The better the question, the better the answer. Here are some guidelines to help you improve your questioning process.

1. Demonstrate your curiosity about how their business operates and your desire to have more than just a cursory understanding of how things are done there.

2. You must be able to answer the following questions. How does this company make money? Who are their customers? What are the competitive challenges the company faces on an ongoing basis?

3. Ask questions about the organization. How is it structured? Who are its key customers? Who are its suppliers? What is the company doing to grow its share in the marketplace?

4. Ask questions about your customers' roles in their organizations and get a sense of context as to how they relate to overall corporate objectives. When you understand their roles in the organization better, it will give you a clearer window into the organization itself.

5. Ask questions about words, phrases or ideas that don't make sense to you. Every industry and company has it's own unique jargon or terminology that makes sense to your customer, but may not be clear to you. Conversely, your company may have terms that you need to make more understandable for your customer.

Pareto at Work

As salespeople, we are all familiar with the Pareto Principle which states that roughly 80% of the effects come from 20% of the causes. In sales teams this means that 20% of your customers generate 80% of your revenues. This is a great rule for conducting a sales interview as well. Salespeople should spend about 20% of the time talking and 80% of the time listening. What tends to happen in many sales situations is the saleperson neglects to pre-plan the sales call and then falls back into old selling habits. We spend too much time talking about our product or service, either by reviewing a glossy brochure or reciting from memory all of the features and benefits of our product or service. You might be talking to a nodding, smiling face on the other side of the desk, but you're not doing anything that will help to establish trust and forge a relationship.

Question Categories

Most salespeople know how to ask questions, but very few work from a comprehensive set of categories that help to guide them and focus their efforts. Becoming an expert at applying the Question Protocol involves learning these categories and continually building upon them and adjusting as circumstances dictate. Let's take a closer look at these categories of questions that will give you all the tools needed to make the Question Protocol really work for you. One category is not any more important than another, but when combined together, questions from each of these categories will serve as very effective prompters for meaningful conversations.

By breaking down your questions into specific categories, you'll be able to pick and choose the best questions for each unique selling scenario. The primary objective of this section is to help you develop and ask questions that move you closer to confirming the business. They are arranged in different categories that will help you initiate contact and build trust with your prospect.

The question categories will help you:

- Determine what the prospect or customer does – his or her role in the organization.

- Plan the next steps or action items with the customer.
- Identify customer stress points.
- Create interest and build credibility.
- Identify which presentation to use with the customer.
- Identify and handle customer resistance.
- Assist in formalizing the decision to use your product or service.
- Negotiate the best deal possible.

No Magic Question

It is important to remember that selling is a process and can often be a complex one. There is no single question that can be recited from memory that will secure the deal for you. It's the careful layering of a variety of questions and their cumulative effect that will win the business. Well-thought-out and intelligent questions that are part of a larger process can and will help you win more business. Prospects and customers only buy what makes sense to them. That's why we focus on providing only make-sense solutions. The majority of your sales efforts should be devoted to the careful and meticulous preparation of your client's solution prior to its presentation. To accomplish this, you need to prepare a series of questions that you can use to uncover what is really going on in their worlds and encourage them to share information with you that will allow you to improve your closing ratios.

Okay, let's examine some of the question categories and what kinds of questions you might ask in a typical selling scenario. Again, these are to serve as guides to get you thinking in the right direction. Every industry and segment will have its own special nuances. Your job will be to add your own questions to continuously improve your Question Protocol inventory.

Opening Questions

When you first meet with your new opportunity, it will be essential for you to build rapport and make a connection. Failure to do so will typically result in a short meeting and a lost opportunity. Here are some simple rules to help you build rapport and trust quickly.

1. Be authentic and genuine – Customers can sense really quickly if you are being disingenuous. Don't be anything that you are not; make sure your sales persona is in alignment with who you really are. Dress appropriately, relax, smile and approach your opportunity with a good attitude and good things will happen.

2. Be open and friendly – Make eye contact, give a firm (not bone-crushing) handshake, approach each opportunity with an expectation of a positive outcome and you'll be well on your way. When you are warm and open, they will be too.

3. Demonstrate interest and curiosity – Most people, especially corporate executive types, are self-focused and love to talk about themselves. This is important to note because we need to find ways to get the prospect to open up and talk to us so that we can identify an area where we can provide a solution. When you are genuinely interested in them and show authentic curiosity, they will be more likely to open up to you and provide information that will be useful.

4. Don't appear desperate – Rapport can't be forced. Don't appear too needy. We all want to be liked, however you shouldn't be seen as trying too hard. When we are overly friendly, too pushy or act in a subservient way, we signal to the customer that we are needy.

5. Be complimentary – If you can find something complimentary to say that's genuine, then say it. Real compliments are endearing and will help you build rapport. You might compliment them on a particular product or service, their office, website, etc. Pay attention to any particularly obvious opportunities.

6. Transition when appropriate – There is always a fine balance between chit-chatting for too long and not spending enough time in the rapport-building part of the selling process. New salespeople often mistakenly feel they have to spend the entire sales call getting their point across with very little time spent developing rapport. Other salespeople spend too much time trying to build rapport and end up aggravating the prospect. If you pay attention to your customers' body language, they will give you visible signs that will let you know they are ready to proceed to the business part of the meeting. If you don't read it right, they may need to be more direct with you to get on with the meeting.

7. Understand their culture – I'm not talking about changing you and your organization to fit each customer, but it definitely helps to understand the culture of the organization you're dealing with. For example, if they are formal by nature and the C-level executives dress in suits and ties, then you might want to do the same and avoid wearing your favorite sports jersey. A quick phone call to the receptionist or executive's assistant will reveal the cultural style of the organization.

Know the Purpose

The primary purpose of the first meeting with your prospect is to establish some trust and build rapport. Each situation is a little different and it is helpful to have an arsenal of questions that you can use to open up your sales conversations.

The objective here is to ask questions around something that both of you can relate to. It might mean talking about the surroundings, the view from their window, etc. The key here is not to rush the prospect or customer. If the customer has not said anything yet, or has made only brief polite remarks, then you are not ready to begin the business part of your meeting. Remember, the sales process should unfold naturally, step by step. Don't expect to transition into the information gathering stages of the sales process without establishing a baseline of commonality and rapport. Let the prospect set the pace. You can do this more effectively if you understand the difference between rapport questions and business questions. Some rapport building questions might include:

- *How was your weekend? Anything exciting?*
- *How's business?*
- *Is that your family in that photo?*
- *How long have you been with XYZ Company?*
- *How did you come to work here?*
- *How did you decide to take the big step of launching your company?*
- *Why did you take your company public?*

Whenever you're dealing with senior executives and entrepreneurs, encourage them to talk about themselves. People who are high achievers and attain leadership positions within their organizations tend to be self-focused. They like to talk about themselves, so don't hesitate to ask them questions about their favorite topic! These questions might appear pretty basic and a bit banal, but that's perfectly okay at this stage. The goal is to ultimately create positive feelings and illicit emotional reactions with your customer.

Transition Questions

Eventually, if you are paying attention, you will receive clues from the prospect or customer that signal their readiness to begin the business part of the meeting. Some customers don't like the small talk and will give you indicators of this very early in the process. Others can spend hours talking about non-business issues. The following questions will help you manage the transition from rapport questions to business questions:

- *Before we get started, would it be helpful if I gave you a little more background about our company?*
- *Would it be helpful if I told you a little bit more about the work we did for XYZ Company?*
- *Would it be useful to you, if I gave you a brief overview of what*

we usually do during this meeting?

- *Have you ever worked with a company like ours before?*

Once again, there is no single question that will be appropriate to open the meeting with every time. That is why we need an inventory of questions that we can draw upon. It's important, however, to always keep the question interesting, otherwise you risk veering off base or asking a question so vague that it's meaningless and you'll risk irritating your prospect. The point of the questions is to be curious. The more curious you are, the better your initial interviews will be. The more information you uncover, the deeper the relationship gets. People will share more detailed and accurate information with people they trust.

Here are some examples of questions that will help you uncover important information:

- *Have you ever reached out to a company like ours before? Who was it? What made you choose them?*
- *What is the primary objective for this month/quarter/year?*
- *What is your CEO's/President's/Boss's primary objective for this month/this quarter/this year?*
- *What made you decide to call us?*
- *Who are your primary competitors?*
- *How does your company distinguish itself in an industry like this?*
- *How do you set yourself apart from the competition?*
- *How do you sustain a competitive edge in an industry as tough as this one?*
- *What are you doing now to deal with the competitive pressures that your salespeople face in today's marketplace?*

Inbound Telephone Questions

Either through referrals or your marketing efforts, the prospect or customer may at times initiate a call to you. People generally don't go to the trouble of inquiring unless there is an interest at some level, so these are great calls to receive. Here are some questions to help you determine the motivation for their call:

- *Thanks for getting in touch. Just out of curiosity, what made you decide to call?*
- *May I ask how you heard about us?*
- *Have you ever thought about working with us before?*
- *What made you decide to take action in this area?*
- *What made you decide to get a quote for this project?*

Technology Questions

The purpose of technology questions is to get some idea of the customer's current level of understanding and to position your company as a leader in innovation. Some customers don't require the latest technologies or see value in them, so the objective is to explore these issues with your customer prior to making any solution suggestions. Some examples might be:

- *Are you aware of some of the latest product innovations in technology in our industry?*
- *Are you familiar with the latest service-related technologies we're seeing in the market and their applications for our industry?*
- *Does technology give your company a competitive advantage? If so, how?*
- *When a new technology enters the marketplace, is your company an early adopter or do you have a wait-and-see policy?*
- *How does your technology differ from your competition?*
- *Independent of cost, if you could improve anything about your technology, what would you do?*
- *Do you have a process for certifying or testing new technologies?*
- *What do you like most (or least) about your current technology?*
- *How are decisions around technology made?*

Quantity Questions

Quantity questions are designed to give you an understanding of how big of an opportunity this customer represents. It will help you determine where to place them in your priority list. For example, you may try asking questions like:

- *How many people does your company employ?*
- *How many offices do you have?*
- *How many of these widgets do you produce annually?*
- *What is your current annual growth rate?*
- *Is your market currently expanding or contracting?*

All of these questions give you some sense of the magnitude of this customer. Some other examples may include:

- *Does your company have plans for expansion in the future?*
- *Have you had any reductions in your team recently?*
- *Where is your customer base located?*
- *How are you staying competitive?*
- *Are you doing business domestically and internationally?*
- *Is your business currently growing or contracting?*
- *How big in dollar volume is your industry?*
- *Have you determined your market share?*

Operational Questions

This question category will help you illuminate the operational considerations for the customer and alleviate concerns or uncertainty about the operational expectations of your product. Basically, you're trying to get a sense of how things work with your customer. The nature of these questions is to get a sense of how they run their business on a day-to-day basis. Questions here might include:

- *How are decisions regarding this type of product determined?*
- *Can you outline for me the procurement process?*
- *Besides yourself, who will be responsible for making this decision?*
- *Who is responsible for quality control?*

- *How are new products or processes evaluated?*
- *Who determines the budgets for operations?*
- *Does your company actively pursue optimization strategies?*
- *How often do you review your current procedures?*

Competitive Questions

The object of competitive questions is to determine where you and your solution stand with the customer. Answers to these questions will give you some insight into your competition in the marketplace and how your products compare. Ideally, you would like to know if your customers have been shopping and who they are comparing you to. Ask these questions to get a sense of your competitive environment:

- *What other solutions are you currently considering?*
- *Who is currently providing these products or services to you?*
- *What have you seen that you liked so far?*
- *Was there anything that you didn't like?*
- *How long have they been your current provider?*
- *Who did you use before them?*
- *Why did you switch?*

Again, ask any question that will give you a sense of who you are competing against.

Budget Questions

Budget questions are helpful in identifying your buyer's expectations and their overall awareness of the total ownership costs of your solution. Ideally, you are trying to determine as much as you can about how budgets are created, how much is in the budget and whether your solution will work within the financial parameters. You might ask something such as:

- *Are you aware of the different ranges of value with our solution?*
- *Is price your primary purchasing criteria? If not, what is your criteria?*

- *Have you determined a budget range that you're comfortable with?*
- *How familiar are you with the overall costs involved in keeping your solution operational?*
- *If we were to find you a solution that perfectly met your needs but was just outside your budget range, would you even want me to present it to you?*

Timing Questions

Timing questions are about determining when the customer is prepared to make the purchase. We can't appear to be too anxious to make a sale or we risk appearing desperate, with our interests outweighing those of our customer. To get a sense of a customer's timing, you could ask:

- *Have you determined an ideal time frame for the delivery of your widget?*
- *What are the specific timelines for this project?*
- *If you were to find a solution that exactly met your requirements and was within your budget, were you looking to have it installed late spring or early summer?*

The strategy behind this last question is to take them out in the calendar as far as reasonably possible. If they are interested in a shorter delivery time frame they will bring you back in the calendar with statements such as, *"We need it sooner than later"* or, *"We were thinking sometime in the spring"*. If you suggest a delivery date too close, you may appear overeager and desperate. Here are a few other questions you might include:

- *If we decided to work together, what would the calendar for that look like?*
- *What does your average sales cycle look like?*
- *Does your company have peak selling or delivery times?*
- *When is your fiscal year-end?*
- *What are the timelines for decisions of this nature?*

Expectation Questions

Expectation questions are designed to get an understanding of customers expectations regarding value and service as well as what they can expect from you as a solution provider. It will also give you an opportunity to add additional value. For example, you might ask:

- *If you could create the perfect vendor relationship, what would that look like?*
- *If there is a product malfunction, what are your service expectations?*
- *If something goes wrong with the quality or delivery of the product, what do you expect to occur? What are your supplier expectations?*

Solution Impact Questions

Solution impact questions are designed to help you gauge the level of impact your solution will have on your customer's organization. They will also cause the customer to reflect on the implications of a solution or how action and inaction will affect them. Questions such as:

- *How will this initiative affect your salespeople?*
- *How will this project impact your marketing?*
- *How will this project affect operations?*
- *Does this project have any impact on recruiting or retention efforts?*
- *How important are repeat sales to your company?*
- *What are you doing to retain your best customers?*
- *How do you plan on implementing this?*
- *What is your company doing to improve their profile in the marketplace?*
- *Can I tell you what some of your counterparts that we have been working with are concerned about?*
- *Can I share with you how some of my other customers in the industry have dealt with this challenge?*
- *Can I tell you how we handled this situation with another customer?*

- *Can I tell you how my manager dealt with this when faced with a similar situation?*

Next Step Questions

Sales professionals know that they should never leave a sales meeting without first attempting to secure an appointment for the next meeting. You can really determine the customer's level of interest by which next-step activities they're willing to commit to. If they're not willing to make some kind of commitment to meet or at least speak with you at some time in the near future, such as the next couple of weeks, then they should not be included in your forecast. A great barometer to gauge their level of interest is to follow up with an outline meeting. If the first meeting went well, then it makes sense to have a follow-up meeting to outline possible solutions or courses of action. If the meeting didn't go well, the prospect will be hesitant or resistant to meeting again to discuss the outline. To assess the customer's interest in a second meeting, ask questions such as:

- *Can we meet next Thursday at 2:30 so that I can show you an outline of how I think we might be able to work together?*
- *I think we're both on the same page here. I'd like to go back to my office and share some of your concerns and challenges with my team and get their insights on how we might prepare a course of action that makes sense. I don't think we're at the proposal stage yet, but I'd like to prepare an outline for you. Why don't we meet next Wednesday at 11:00 a.m. so that I can share with you some of our initial thinking? I'd also like to meet with some of your other team members to help develop the solution more fully. Does that make sense to you?*

Resistance Questions

Objections and resistance are a natural part of the sales process. When many salespeople receive a negative response, they often try to overcome the objection using some time-tested tactic or worse, they stop trying and just move on to the next opportunity. Here are some questions that will help you move forward in the sales process:

- *Thank you for your candor, but I'm surprised to hear you respond that way. I find in most cases, people are open to meeting further and taking a look at potential solutions. Just out of curiosity, what would be holding you back from that?*
- *Would it be helpful if I set up a conference call so that you could talk to a number of our customers?*
- *Would you consider attending one of our company events?*
- *When can you come and tour our facility?*
- *Can I get a tour of your facility?*
- *What if we did an online presentation for your key people?*
- *Why don't you and I meet with my boss?*
- *Why don't you and I meet with our technical experts?*
- *Why don't we get our technical people together?*
- *What do you think is our next step?*
- *Who do you think I should speak with next?*
- *Would you like me to keep you informed?*

Working with Committees

In today's marketplace, you will often find that companies use committees to make many of their purchasing decisions, particularly if the purchase is large or involves any level of risk. You will often hear these kinds of responses. *"Let me run this by the committee and see what they think about it"* or, *"This needs to get run past the committee"* or, *"The committee makes most of these decisions in this area"* or, *"This will have to get approved by the committee, but it's just a formality."* Here are some questions to help you get past this obstacle:

- *Would it be helpful to make a presentation directly to the committee/work group?*
- *That's interesting. Just out of curiosity, why wouldn't you want*

me to present before the group?
- *How does the committee work?*
- *What is the committee's decision-making process?*
- *Who would we be presenting to?*
- *How is the committee formed?*
- *What is the best way to communicate with the people on the committee?*

The key with committees is to be fully prepared prior to the presentation. This means doing what is necessary to communicate with all the members of the group before your meeting. This may require a variety of face-to-face meetings, phone calls or emails. The bigger the opportunity, the more time you will need to invest.

Elaboration Questions

Elaboration questions are designed to get the customer or prospect talking. They give you more information or details regarding specific needs and will help uncover opportunities. Here are some examples of how we can add some depth to our standard questions:

- **Standard Question:** *Who will be responsible for the decision to purchase?*
- **Elaboration Question:** *Can you walk me through your organization's decision-making process?*
- **Standard Question:** *Are you happy with your current production work flow process?*
- **Elaboration Question:** *Share with me your level of satisfaction with your current production work flow process?*
- **Standard Question:** *What do you like most about your current provider?*
- **Elaboration Question:** *Could you describe for me the attributes you look for in your supplier relationships?*

Elaboration questions usually begin with:
- *Describe for me...*

- *Share with me...*
- *Explain for me...*
- *Walk me through how...*
- *Tell me how/about...*

One of the advantages of elaboration questions is that they demonstrate to your customer that you are truly interested in them and willing to listen to their responses.

It's important to note that elaboration questions should be used strategically and not for every question. Go through your question inventory and carefully select which questions would work best for each unique selling situation.

Implication Questions

Your goal as a sales professional is to identify the problems or challenges a customer faces and then help develop solutions that take care of them. For a solution to motivate the customer, the problem must be quantified. In other words, how much is inaction costing the customer? Most customers don't apply this level of analysis to their challenges. Your job is to get them to discover how much money, time, and resources are being wasted by not addressing the issue. The following questions lead the customer to think about implications:

- *What do you think this issue is costing you?*
- *How does this issue affect your overall profitability?*
- *How does this issue affect your productivity?*
- *How does this issue affect your quality control?*
- *How is this problem impacting the bottom line?*
- *How much effort is required to look after this problem?*
- *How does this issue affect your costs?*
- *Have you lost customers over this issue? If so, what were those customers worth to you?*
- *How does this issue impact other areas of your business?*
- *What will be the cost to you if we delay another day/month/year?*

- *How has this issue affected corporate morale?*
- *How much does it cost you to find and train a new employee?*
- *Will this issue have an impact on your corporate objectives?*

Buyer Questions

Questions can go both ways and it's important to try to anticipate any questions your customers may typically have and be ready to pre-emptively address them. In any sales situation, make sure you are addressing these unspoken questions that are often in the mind of the buyer.

- *Does this solution make sense?*
- *What is the real cost?*
- *Is this a good deal for me or my company?*
- *Can I purchase this cheaper elsewhere?*
- *Will this company live up to its promises?*
- *Does this salesperson understand our issues and challenges?*

We can't always control how buyers answer these questions, but we can exert a degree of influence over the questions they ask themselves.

Whoever is asking the questions is controlling the conversation. The important part for the seller is to not only ask high-value questions, but to demonstrate to the buyer that you are actually listening to the answers. We must actively listen to their responses so that we may ask another question that will keep them talking.

A Strong Arsenal

By now, I'm sure you've come to understand the importance of building a strong arsenal of high-value questions and asking them in a carefully layered sequence. If employed consistently and effectively, the Question Protocol will become the very foundation of all your sales efforts. You'll be able to build relationships of trust more quickly, uncover your customers' needs and be in a better position to provide solutions that make sense.

What's Next

Even when you've carefully prepared a thoughtful group of questions from your category list and asked them in the properly structured sequence to help your customers make more informed decisons, there will inevitably be times when you continue to encounter buyer resistance. There's no way to completely eliminate resistance so you need to be prepared to deal with it. We'll explore the causes of buyer resistance in our next chapter and what you can do to help your customers get past any hurdles. You'll learn how to help them develop the certainty they need to make smarter and more confident purchasing decisions.

CHAPTER 8

Handling Buyer Resistance

The sun comes up in the morning and sets at night. Taxes have to be paid. No one lives forever. These are a few of life's undeniable realities. You can add to that list the fact that you're not going to sell everyone.

"We really appreciated you taking the time to present your solutions to us. Unfortunately we've decided to move in a different direction."

"The information your team provided was very useful, but we've decided to back away from this project for the time being."

"We thought your solution was viable, however the team decided to use a different vendor."

"We would love to work with you, but our Vice President has a relationship with another vendor."

Everyday Occurrences

These phrases and others like them are everyday occurrences for sales professionals. If you've been selling for any length of time then you've no doubt heard them yourself. Many of your potential customers just won't buy from you no matter how amazing the opportunity is or how skilled you are at presenting it to them. This won't change regardless of all the wonderful strategies you may try to employ. Every sales person knows this, but here's where I'm going to suggest something that you may not have given enough thought to before.

Differences

There's a difference between an *absolute no* and mere resistance; quite a big difference in fact. An *absolute no* is a dead end, there's no way around it and you just have to accept it, no matter how frustrating that may be. Resistance, however, doesn't necessarily mean *no*. Many times it simply means, not yet. Think of it as a yellow light instead of a red light. Buyer resistance is a natural part of every sales professional's daily life, but it shouldn't mean that you automatically abandon a potential opportunity and move on to the next. If you make the mistake of prematurely interpreting initial resistance as an *absolute no*, then you may very well be walking away from potential profit. Often times, the purchasing process represents some type of change for the buyer and, as we're all aware, change is a difficult proposition for the vast majority of the population. Getting your customers to embrace the change your solution may present is a big part of your role as a trusted advisor.

Think of it this way. You're traveling by car to an important meeting and for some reason your originally planned route isn't available and a detour is necessary; a detour that will result in it taking longer to reach your destination. So what do you do? Do you abandon your trip and go home because of the detour? Of course not. You simply alter your original expectations, take the detour route, adjusting and adapting as necessary along the way. Is it inconvenient? Absolutely, but so is life. Just another one of those realities you have to deal with.

Temporary Roadblocks

You need to think of buyer resistance as a temporary roadblock. Resistance is rarely a dead end on its own. It's just a signal that a change in direction may be needed. It signals that you need to detour and find an alternate route to the sale, other than the one you may have originally planned. Sometimes the detour route won't work out and you'll hit a dead end, but many times it will work out just fine.

You'll learn things along the way as well that may help you change the way you plan your original route for the future. Negative feedback is actually incredibly useful because it allows us to correct our course and avoid pitfalls that we may not otherwise have known existed. So we need to embrace it, rather than run from it.

Resistance or Hesitation?

There's another important delineation that's essential for you to understand – there's a difference between *resistance* and *hesitation*. Knowing which is actually taking place at any given time during the purchasing process is a key factor in confirming more sales. Buyer hesitation is very often the outward manifestation of a need for more information. When it comes right down to it, the decision to purchase requires a good deal of confidence on the part of the buyer, especially when the purchase is larger in size and scope. Confidence makes it easier to pull the trigger. A lack of confidence doesn't mean that customers won't eventually purchase, rather it means that they haven't yet reached the level of confidence needed to make the decision painless. Your job is to supply the information that will take them to the level they need to be at to say y*es*. This is why we spend so much time developing a Question Protocol. Good questions will help you discover what may be the root cause of any apparent hesitation and keep the deal moving forward. Developing a strong level of rapport during the question and information gathering phase of the sales process will also help you to increase the level of confidence your buyer has with any proposed solutions that will follow. When buyers feel that you have their interests at heart, they'll be more likely to answer your questions more thoughtfully and perceive you as competent and trustworthy.

So when you sense that you're getting push back during a sales opportunity, your first question to yourself should be, *"Is this resistance or is it merely hesitation?"* It may take a little time at first before you become adept at recognizing the difference, but when you do, you'll find that you'll be far less likely to abandon a still worthy opportunity. In addition, you'll also know better when to cut bait and move along. No one wants to devote unnecessary time to a prospect that is overly resistant. One of the biggest mistakes a sales professional can make is trying too hard to resurrect a prospect that has no real intention of purchasing. Being able to accurately discern the difference between resistance and hesitation will go a long way in helping you to avoid this time-wasting trap.

Ask the Question

If you've developed a good level of initial rapport with your customer, you may find it useful in many cases to simply broach the subject outright. Here's how you might position it:

"Before we go any further, Ms. Prospect, I just want to make sure that I'm not missing anything that you may be concerned about. I'm sensing a bit of hesitation or maybe even resistance and wanted to give you the opportunity to set me straight on what might be causing that if that's the case."

By asking customers for feedback at this point, you're showing them that you're sensitive to their needs and want to make sure you arrive at the solution that makes the most sense for their individual requirements. Their responses will help you accurately determine if their concerns are more related to hesitation or resistance. Either way, you'll definitely be in a better position to address any issues because there's no guessing on your part; the customer is identifying the issues for you. When they have questions and concerns, educate them. When they don't understand, discover the source of their misunderstanding and clarify things. As you do, their levels of confidence will start to rise and any pain associated with making the purchasing decision begins to fade away.

Managing the Pace

Resistance can also come from a salesperson moving the sales process along at a pace that is uncomfortable for the customer. You need to remember that the new sales model we discussed earlier has suggested your protocol should involve 40% of your time being devoted to building rapport and 30% to listening. This ensures that the pace of the sale is more about making the customer comfortable about the process and your intent rather than simply pushing things to the confirmation stage as quickly as possible. This initial, up-front time positions you differently than the average salesperson and that alone can help to eliminate inherent resistance barriers. Your job is to direct the sales process in a way that ensures that you still maintain control, but not in a way that makes the customer feel uncomfortable. When you follow the process laid out in our new sales model, you'll always be in control of the proceedings. You won't get lost along the way, get off track or miss out on opportunities. And best of all, you'll be reducing the level of inherent resistance many salespeople have to deal with simply because the steps in the new sales model are specifically designed to reduce hesitation and resistance in a natural, unobtrusive fashion.

The Worth of a No

One way to ensure that you don't spend too much time worrying about the *no* factor is to actually determine the worth of a *no*. In almost every case, a *no* can be profitable if you're looking at the situation from the right point of view.

Here's what I mean. Let's assume that I close a sale on one out of every four presentations I make – a 1 to 3 ratio – and these are consistent numbers for me. And let's assume, for our demonstration's sake, that a closed sale is worth $5000. Most people would look at this and say the sale is worth $5000 and a *no* is worth zero, but that's not the way I look at it. In my books, it takes 4 presentations to make $5000; those are my numbers. That means each of those presentations is actually worth $1250. It takes me four presentations to make my $5000 with each one representing the exact same net worth of $1250 regardless of the outcome. In my world, a *no* is just as valuable as a *yes* because I know I need to hear *no* three times before I arrive at a *yes*. It's all in how you look at things when you know your numbers. This keeps my spirits and confidence high and ensures that I'm eager to make my next presentation, even if my last one crashed and burned, simply because I know I'm that much closer to a *yes*. Every *no* I get means $1250 in my pocket.

Anticipating Resistance

Preparation is the key to being in the strongest position to handle resistance. A highly effective planning discipline that Rainmakers implement involves identifying all the negative responses that could conceivably be encountered and then forming pre-emptive questions that effectively prevent these barriers from showing up later. Here's what you don't want to happen: You've done all your homework for your client. You've prepared a perfect solution, presented it masterfully and are now just waiting for the customer to enthusiastically present you with a purchase order. But rather than applaud your brilliance, the customer now tells you that your perfect solution isn't in the budget! This all-too-often encountered scenario could have easily been pre-vented by anticipating budget resistance back in the Question Protocol portion of the sales process. Before you ever start to prepare a solution, you could ask a question such as, *"Has a budget been determined for this project and if so, what would the ceiling be?"* And price resistance is just one of many potential roadblocks you could anticipate and prepare for. What about timing resistance? Or delivery challenges? After-sale service expectations? The list goes on. The point is that by applying a small measure of planning discipline, you can develop pre-emptive questions that will expose potential areas of resistance that you can address in your solutions before they become barriers later on.

All in a Day

At the end of the day, the important thing to remember is that hesitation, resistance and an absolute no, are all part of the professional salesperson's daily reality. While you always want to do everything you can to eliminate or mitigate their occurrences, it's essential that you don't let them impact your attitude and long-term confidence. Always remember that sales is a numbers game with the odds almost always stacked against you. That doesn't mean that you can't have an incredibly successful career in spite of this uphill arrangement; it just means that you have to be realistic and be able to roll with the punches when things don't go your way. If ultimately you strike out despite all your best efforts, move on. Another appearance at the plate is another opportunity to hit it out of the park. But you have to be willing to step back up and not let the last strikeout phase you or it will hinder your next at bat. Play ball!

What's Next

One of the things Rainmakers have come to understand is that old-fashioned *cold calling* is not only tough to bring yourself to do on a consistent basis, it's actually a very inefficient approach to prospecting. In our next chapter, I'll introduce you to a different way of approaching new business opportunities; one that's less painful to implement and way more effective in opening new doors for you and your company.

CHAPTER 9

Target Niche Marketing

If you ever played with a magnifying glass then you understand first-hand the power of focus. A magnifying glass works by taking everyday sunshine and focusing it to a single point. This concentration of energy is so strong that it can actually burn things and start fires.

When we apply this same level of focus and concentration in the marketplace, our results can be equally powerful. An easy way to determine where you're focused is to look at where you're concentrating your new business acquisition efforts. Are you focused on any specific segment or are you fishing all over the marketplace? Casting your line here, there and everywhere that you see the occasional fish jump? Do you move from one market to the next where you see activity or perhaps you're simply chasing the competition? When this is the case, more often than not, your efforts are not the result of any kind of strategic focus. You're merely being reactionary; always hunting for the next hotspot.

Creating Focus

To improve our sales results, we need to be better at focusing our efforts. No more guessing. We need to start fishing where the fish are and concentrating our efforts to produce better results in less time. We need to market to strategically targeted niches or segments. We can define Target Niche Marketing as, 'Partitioning the marketplace into identifiable segments or groups of people who network and communicate with one another.' The key words here are *identifiable, network* and *communicate.* In other words, you need to look for networking patterns within definable segments.

Your Starting Point

Let me show you a great place to start. If you were to look at this as a step-by-step process, the first step we would take would be to look at your existing customers. Look at last year's customers, the last two year's customers and even as far back as your last three year's customers. Look at who's been buying from you. Once you've identified who *has* been buying from you, you can then figure out who *hasn't* been buying from you.

The next step is to identify which specific markets these customers are active in. In other words, identify each niche you're currently working in through the customers you already have. Start putting your customers into buckets. Each bucket represents a market segment or niche. These could be specific sectors such as banking, insurance, hospitals, long-term care, government, manufacturing, telecommunications, real estate, retail, transportation, legal, oil and gas, food services – wherever your current customers operate.

There are a couple of rules you should consider before you complete this exercise. First of all, you can have as many segments as you want, the number doesn't matter just as long as they're identified. Secondly, a market or segment can be big or small – it doesn't matter. But, here's something important to remember: **Smaller the Niche, Bigger the Market**. Let's discuss exactly what I mean by that.

The Advantage of Specialized Niches

When a niche is small, it's often because it's very specialized. There aren't as many players in the niche because it is so specialized. When niches are specialized they tend to be more profitable as well. For instance, who do you think makes more money – the dentist or the orthodontist? One is a more specialized field than the other and therefore often commands a higher price in the marketplace. Who do you think does the marketing for the orthodontist? You guessed it - the dentist! So the question to ask is, *"How do we get the market to do the marketing?"* The bottom line here is that the more you're perceived as a specialist in the niche, the more the market or customers will do the marketing for you. If you can truly specialize in the distinct needs (real or perceived) of the niche and position yourself accordingly, you can own the segment. Once you have experience and credibility with one company in the niche, then the others become much easier to bring into the fold. The old adage, 'birds of a feather, flock together' comes to mind, so remember, **Smaller the Niche, Bigger the Market**. Once you have identified the niches that you work in, the next step is to work each niche *horizontally and vertically*. Let's investigate both parts of this strategy individually.

Working Horizontally

Working a niche *horizontally* means targeting as many other companies as possible that also operate in that market niche. These are the competitors of the companies you currently do business with. Because you're already working with someone in the niche, you'll automatically have increased credibility with other companies in the same niche. Your direct experience in their market sector gives you an immediate advantage. It accomplishes two things for you.

First, customers are always impressed with directly related experience. It provides a sense of security and gives them a strong, tangible benefit that will help them rationalize choosing to do business with you. Secondly, it eliminates a barrier that is often constructed as an easy way to dismiss a potential service provider. No experience, no consideration. The more companies you work with in their market niche, the better! And the more directly related the experience, better yet. For instance, if your identified market niche is restaurants and you're trying to close a deal with an Italian restaurant, the only thing better than direct restaurant experience is direct *Italian* restaurant experience. This experience positions you as an expert or specialist in the eyes of the customer. And here's why. Customers always think that their specific needs are different than anyone else's. That may be true on occasion, but most of the time it's not. But *they think it's true* and that's all that really matters. Remember, perceptions shape reality. Your direct experience makes you appear to be a specialist, an *expert* on their industry. You may never have actually worked in an Italian restaurant, but your experience dealing with others in the niche makes you *appear* to be an expert on their subject matter and that perception gives you an advantage over the generalist every time.

Remember, you don't necessarily need to become an in-depth expert in their business, but you need to understand their issues and how your business relates to theirs.

An Italian Restaurant

Here's an example of how you might position yourself in the restaurant industry and to an Italian restaurant in particular:

"Mr. Customer, at XYZ Restaurant Supplies we have direct experience in working with many different types of restaurants. We've worked with Company A, Company B, Company C and many others, but we believe that every restaurant category has it's own unique set of needs and challenges. XYZ specializes in providing solutions to the restaurant industry and my particular area of focus happens to be in the specific needs of Italian restaurants."

Now, are their needs *really* different than other restaurants? Probably not, but they think they are and that's what's important. Given a choice, people would rather deal with a specialist than a generalist. Always. Every time. Particularly when everything else is equal. So positioning yourself as a specialist in their particular market will give you a distinct advantage over your competition. It's just how we think as human beings – it's our nature. And if you know how to leverage typical human behavioral tendencies, your results will speak for themselves.

Customers as Marketers

One of the benefits of being perceived as a niche specialist, is that your customers will even start to market for you. They become your advocates and will talk to others in their specific market niche. Companies within segments talk to each other – at trade shows, industry events and conferences. They often share the same market issues and the same challenges. They often ask each other for advice. You will often hear, *"We have that same challenge too. What did you guys do to fix it? Who do you work with? Anybody you would recommend?"* People feel better about recommending a specialist they do business with than they do recommending a generalist. It makes them appear to be very strategic and intelligent. People in the know don't work with just anybody, they work with specialists! Again, it's predictable human behavior.

Working Vertically

Now, after you looked at every opportunity to work a niche horizontally, it's time to start working it deep or *vertically*. This means looking at all the various companies that work with or partner with your customers. These are all the companies that supply services, products or materials to your customers. For instance, if you do business with a printing company, then working the printing niche deep or vertically would mean you would target paper companies, ink manufacturers, equipment suppliers and transportation companies. The rule is simple, anyone who does business with your current customer is part of the vertical market. Everyone in your customers' food chain can be included. Again, this works to enhance your credibility factor. When you work a niche deep, you immediately move from *untested entity* status to the higher ground of *proven supplier* by virtue of your association with someone the potential customer knows and trusts. Working the niche deep gives you an introduction that makes your sales calls *warm* instead of *cold*. Your trust connection gets a head start and it makes your job easier.

Existing Customer Referrals

You can make working the niche deep even more effective by getting referrals from your existing customers. This is called third party endorsement and it's always more effective than just a salesperson's word. Company advertising, marketing and promotional materials are great, but your customers often view them more as hype than reality. This is why a referral from a known and trusted source is so effective – it helps to support and verify the claims you're making in your sales information. Here's how you might position a call to someone in your customer's niche:

"Good morning, Ms. Prospect, my name is Michael Vickers and I'm an optimization specialist with XYZ in our Graphics division. We specialize in the printing industry. I've been working with Sam Smith over at ABC Printing and during the course of working with Sam, your name came up as someone who might also be interested in the type of solutions we're providing to ABC. The reason for my call Ms. Prospect, is to see if I could schedule a 20-minute briefing to meet you personally, show you how we are improving efficiency in the industry with our solutions and then determine if there is anything we should be discussing relative to your business."

Your call now seems to make more sense to your potential customer. It's not just random guessing, but rather a natural progression of the work you've already been doing with their partner company. They can even call your current client to confirm what you're saying is valid. And because you've established a good relationship with your existing customer, you're going to get a great reference. This warms up your first meeting even further and accelerates the time it takes to establish trust with the new customer.

Working your niches vertically is a great strategy for increasing your overall effectiveness and will have a real positive impact on your call-to-close ratios. Not all of the companies you identify when you look deep into the niche will make sense for you to call on, but many will and leveraging the association they have with your current customer is one of best strategies available to you. It also allows you to further identify other market segments that may be more profitable for you and your company in the future.

Becoming an Expert

So, how can we appear as experts if we've never actually worked in our client's business? How can we get our clients to market our services for us? How can we elevate our status from that of a generalist to a specialist? Let's take a look at a few very specific strategies to enhance your status as a niche expert.

Niche Stresses

As we've learned in our previous module, you don't have to become an actual expert on your customer's business, only an expert on how your product or service impacts or relates to your customer's business. Find out what issues your niche faces. What are their stresses? A great way to start is with industry trade magazines and websites. Almost every industry has trade magazines and association websites and they're a great source for getting a pulse on the sector. What's current? What are the industry challenges? Gather as much available knowledge as you can to give you insight into their sector. Make sure you interview your current customers in the niche as they will provide you with lots of industry information, jargon and buzzwords, etc. Once you've done your background work, here are three specific strategies you can employ to help enhance your reputation as a niche or segment specialist.

Business Cards

Our first strategy is a simple one that's available to everyone – your business card. If you're like many of our customers whose primary responsibility is sales, the title on your business card probably says something like Sales Representative, Account Representative, Account Manager, Territory Manager or something similar. These types of titles say the same thing to your customer – *salesperson,* which means you're trying to *sell* them something. You're more likely to be perceived as a generalist with this type of title and your products or solutions will be valued as a commodity. Many customers and prospects put up a protective shield when salespeople approach them and this is especially true of professional buyers. When you're a *salesperson* in the eyes of your customers, they employ defensive strategies to manage you.

Your objective is to break down this natural defense mechanism, and a strategically thought-out business card can really set the stage for overcoming this challenge. Your card is often the first introduction of you and your company to your prospective customer. To be an effective strategic tool, it can't be the generic, one-size-fits-all kind of card we see so often. It needs to convey a direct benefit of your service or product to the niche you're working in. Let me give you an example.

If, for instance, your product was water filtration systems and you were targeting restaurants as one of your niches, one of the benefits of your product might be improved water quality as a result of a robust and effective purification system. Instead of describing yourself as an Account Manager, your business card title might introduce you as a *Hospitality Water Purification Specialist.* The title communicates a very specific benefit of the product you provide and positions you as an expert in that particular niche. The key is to get the customer thinking about how working with you might benefit them in ways that they might not normally associate with your product or service. Just remember, the benefit has to be real and authentic – never position yourself as something you're not. But as long as the benefit is real and you can back it up, you'll be viewed differently. Remember, customers usually buy the benefit of the product you're selling rather than the product itself. It's your job to position and sell the benefit. Your business card can set the stage for you right from the start.

It's important that you customize your card according to the niche you're working. If you work in 5 different niches, you might need 5 different cards. Consider your business card a function of marketing, not HR. Just as you would have a product brochure that identifies the value and benefit of your product, your business card is a PR piece. Remember, your customers think their needs are different than anyone else's. And when you position yourself as a specialist in their specific niche, you've positioned yourself above your competition.

When you use it correctly, your business card can be one of the most cost-effective marketing tools your company could ever invest in. You use them already, so why not make them work more effectively for you? It's a small investment that provides great returns.

Web Landing Pages

Another strategic tool you can use to help position you as a niche specialist is to have customized, niche-specific web landing pages designed and produced that you can direct potential customers to. This page wouldn't be accessible to clients coming in through your company's main homepage on the web. Instead, it's a stand-alone link that you would provide only to companies in the specific niche or segment you're targeting. The goal here is to create an ultra-specialized page with its own URL that will feature all the clients you work with that do business in the same niche as the customer you're trying to sell to. And the key here is to be extremely focused. So to use the example of the Italian restaurant, your webpage wouldn't feature all of the restaurants you've worked with, just the Italian restaurants. Remember, **Smaller the Niche, Bigger the Market**. If you ask your current customers for permission, most customers will be more than happy to provide logos, photos, testimonials – whatever you need – so that you can create this special reference page. When potential customers see the logos of the companies you've worked with as well as any applicable photos provided and then read the testimonials and any case studies you may provide, it really cements your positioning as an expert in their niche. And when they see that your experience is pinpoint specific to their individual needs, you're way ahead of your competitors. You will be considered a niche expert. These web pages can then be linked to promotional material, emails, advertisements, etc. If you are unable to create niche specific web pages, simply create niche specific PDF's that look like webpages that have your customers logos, testimonials, etc. You can then send them as an attachment to your email.

Writing Articles

Nothing establishes you personally as an expert more than having your views and opinions published in a respected, independent magazine, journal or newsletter. People believe that authors are experts. Again, it's human nature and you can create instant credibility if you become a published author on a particular subject. Now with many major newspapers and magazines, it's not so easy to get published, but that's not the case with most trade magazines. If you have legitimate subject matter experience and expertise, most trade publications will be happy to publish an article you provide to them as long as it's of specific interest to their audience and it's not a self-promoting advertorial. It's even better if you work for a large reputable firm, as it tends to give more credence and respectability to the publication if they can provide content from industry leaders.

Most trade magazines face a common problem – they're budget poor. They rarely have enough money to commission all the articles they'd like. Here's how you can take advantage of that challenge to help them and yourself out at the same time. In lieu of payment for your article, simply ask them to provide you with a substantial number of copies of the issue in which your article appears. Or, because you own the copyright (always remember to do this), you can reprint the article without publisher permission. Most will be happy to oblige and these copies can be provided to your clients as handouts and "proof of claim" of your expertise in their niche. When they see an article that's written by you in a trade magazine or journal they know and respect, you're now an expert in their eyes.

Ghostwriter Help

If you're a good writer so much the better, but if you're not, don't let that stop you. There are many professional writers who will happily serve as a ghostwriter for a fee. You simply supply them with the subject information and they'll write the article while you maintain full author's rights to the final piece. It's a common practice in the publishing industry and it's a great way to produce a really professional finished piece if you aren't comfortable writing it yourself.

You'd be surprised where authoring articles can take you. The more you write, the more in demand you'll become. Published authors are often in demand as speakers for trade conferences. And like writing, speaking on a specific topic at recognized industry events adds more weight to your position as a niche expert.

Trade Shows

Many companies exhibit at industry trade shows; it's common practice and your own industry expects that you will exhibit in its own shows. Potential customers walk up and down the aisles, moving from booth to booth, filling their bags with literature and handouts from all of the exhibitors which invariably include many of your competitors. Your marketing material gets lost with all of the other corporate information that's being handed out. It's still important to go to industry trade shows, but the following strategy will help establish you and your company as specialists and separate you from the competition.

Once you have fully dissected your niche and understand all of the players in the food chain from suppliers to your customers' customers, you can then determine *what trade shows your customers attend.* Chances are great you won't find any of your competitors there. Let me give you an example of how this might work. One of our clients is a major financial institution and provides a variety of financial services to many market segments. They attend all of the financial services trade shows, which are often crowded with their primary competitors. To apply our trade show strategy, we began by breaking down their customer base into segments. This illustrated to them that they had some clearly defined niches to work with. One of those niches was Radiology. The financial institution had hundreds of radiologists that were clients. The niche was profitable and had lots of potential. Once we knew who they did have as clients within the Radiology niche, it was easy for us to determine who they didn't yet have as clients. We then identified all of the conferences, networking events and trade shows the Radiologists attended and made sure they were at all of the events. And here's the great part – *none* of their competitors were in attendance. It was theirs exclusively. Their positioning literature at the events was focused on the Radiologist and was very specific to their issues. The results were staggering. Our client then applied this strategy to other niches within the medical community and is currently enjoying *preferred provider* status. The point here is this: pay attention to industry shows, but more importantly, exhibit at the shows your customers and prospective customers attend.

I'm confident that once your realize how much more effective and efficient you can become when you utilize Target Niche Marketing as a primary strategy for opening new markets, you will want to adopt this strategy for every market you choose to work in.

What's Next

In our next chapter, we'll explore a highly specialized and lucrative niche that every salesperson should aspire to working in; a niche that has nothing to do with specific industries, but rather *all* industries. That niche is the executive corporate suite or what I like to call the *C-Suite* – the ultimate destination for the Rainmaker. Our next chapter will focus on what you need to know to succesfully penetrate this lofty marketplace, operate profitably once you're there and then maintain your reputation as a C-Suite specialist in the long term.

CHAPTER 10

Selling to the C-Suite

Let's start our chapter with a quick definition of exactly who we're talking about when we refer to the C-Suite. Often times, it's the CEO or Chief Executive Officer of an organization, but it doesn't always have to be. It could be the Chief Operating Officer, the Chief Financial Officer, the Chief Technology Officer or the Chief Marketing Officer. It really depends on the specific company and industry you're targeting. But one thing that all of these individuals have in common is that they're at the highest levels of their organizations – the Corporate Suite or the C-Suite. They're the people in charge of the strategic vision and direction of their divisions and organizations. They're typically less involved in the *engine room* and more involved in the *map* or *chart room*. Their viewpoint of organizational needs is at a higher level and the scope of their overall responsibilities is generally farther reaching than at the lower levels of their companies. The pressure to perform and succeed is the greatest at these levels – the stakes are higher and the ramifications of decisions made here are greater in scope.

Challenges and Rewards

But with greater risk, comes greater reward and C-Suite executives thrive on this challenge. There's no doubt that selling to the C-Suite is a more challenging proposition than selling at lower levels, but when you successfully master the strategies and techniques involved in appealing to this level, the rewards are exponentially greater for you. You'll be far less likely to become constricted by the downward pricing pressures so often found at lower levels of management and far more likely to gain status as a trusted strategic advisor.

Understanding the C-Suite

In order to sell effectively at any level, it's imperative that you know your target audience. This is especially true of the C-Suite, so the perfect place to begin our exploration is with a look into what really drives the C-Suite executive.

More often than not, top level executives are challenged on dual fronts – trying to manage the current demands of today while having to invest equal amounts of time and energy into planning for the inevitable challenges of tomorrow. Both tasks are essential to their success. Responding to known, existing problems is never easy, but trying to predict the future and anticipate potential problems is an even greater challenge. But planning for and avoiding or mitigating problems that haven't yet surfaced is a very real part of the top level executive's far-reaching responsibility. Steering the course for mid-range and long-range destinations is often at the forefront of the C-Suite executive's mandate. Part pragmatist and part futurist, today's C-Suite executive must be a master of problem solving, strategic planning and resource allocation. Staying ahead of industry curves is a measuring stick of executive leadership and those who can assist top executives in charting the course for ongoing success by contributing significant and lasting value can become part of their inner circle.

If you want to gain entry into the inner circle of the C-Suite, you must be able to deliver the kind of value that appeals to the mindset you'll find there. You must see their companies and industries as they do – it's bigger picture thinking and it's the key to C-Suite selling success. You must position your company's value proposition in such a way that it not only addresses the organizational needs of today, but those of the future as well.

The C-Suite Mindset

The personality type of your target customers almost always has a significant impact on how they react to your presentations, so it's really helpful to know the personality traits of the typical C-Suite level executive.

With that in mind, let's take a look at 12 common characteristics of C-Suite leaders.

1. They usually have healthy egos and are high achievers. They see themselves as the best and that's what they expect in return.
2. They seek and have power, control and authority. They welcome this responsibility and have the wherewithal to exercise that power with little or no hesitation.
3. They like communications to be brief, direct and to-the-point. With so many responsibilities to address, they appreciate and admire brevity.
4. They're self-assured, goal-oriented and driven to results. They're front runners who enjoy challenges and the process of reaching difficult destinations.
5. They're accountable and don't run from responsibility. They know the buck stops at their doors and they're comfortable with having the final say.
6. They're highly competitive and passionate about their work. You don't get to the top with knowledge alone – it takes plenty of personal drive and ambition as well.
7. They're always on the lookout for information or wisdom that will give them an edge. You can't be mapping the future without trying to become as informed as possible about the hazards of the journey. They welcome insight that will help them stay ahead and on top.

8. They hate wasting their time, or having someone else waste it for them. Time is a high-level currency for them.

9. They're usually well-read and informed about the industry they work in. Trend spotting and market reaction can't happen unless you stay abreast of what's changing and evolving.

10. Many are early adopters and seek out new ideas and technologies that have yet to be embraced by the general population. Being first is a big part of their personality type.

11. They're not risk adverse – bigger rewards follow bigger risks. They have the intestinal fortitude to take calculated risks – it's what's expected of their positions. Not many top level executives got to where they are by always playing it safe.

12. They like to ask and answer direct questions. Again, it's all about time and efficiency for them. Respect this and you'll be on your way to establishing trust.

Researching

It should go without saying that every sales professional needs to re-search a potential client company before initiating contact. You need to know as much as you can about the company and its industry in order to make a good initial impression. But when you're dealing with the C-Suite, you need to go a step further. There's often quite a bit you can find out about the individual executive you're seeking to meet with well in advance of your meeting.

Unlike many lower level employees, C-Suite executives often are written about in trade publications and even mainstream news because they frequently serve as the go-to spokespeople for their companies and industries. Writers interview them, they quote them and then publish their views to eager audiences.

So make it a discipline to find out as much as you can about the individual as well as his or her company. Often times, they have richly experienced backgrounds that have contributed to them being where they are and these backgrounds are diligently docu-mented by publications and in company-distributed press releases.

Start with a perfunctory Google search on the company itself and then branch out from there. Search the executive's name in both news and image categories. Find out which trade publications cover the tar-geted industry and then search their archives for anything you can find.

Once you've gathered as much information on the company and individual as possible, you should start to get a grasp of the issues the industry as a whole is facing. You can be guaranteed that those same issues will be top of mind in the C-Suite. The more you know about the direct and indirect stresses facing your potential client, the better you'll be able to position your company's value proposition in a way that connects on the executive level. When you understand their problems and challenges, you'll be seen as more than just a sales-person – you actually start to take on the role of an industry analyst. That's the kind of person that gets the attention of the C-Suite.

When They Get Involved

One of the most important things you must be aware of if you want to gain access to the C-Suite is when executives typically become involved in the procurement process. If your timing isn't right, you're almost assuredly going to be dealing with someone at a lower level.

To accurately determine this entry point, you first must understand that purchasing is not something you'll commonly find at the top of the list of responsibilities for most senior executives. More frequent-ly, purchasing is relegated to lower levels of the organization and the procurement process is carried out only after a need is clear-ly established and further strategic input and evaluation is not re-quired. In other words, if you're only getting to the table at the time the purchasing department is sending out requests for information or requests for proposals, then more likely than not, you've already missed your best opportunity to influence the proceedings. The train has left the station and at this point, you'll just be one of the many other vendors who are in reactionary mode, *hoping* they'll be lucky enough to win the business.

Clearly, this is not the optimum time to be trying to convince potential clients of the real value of your company's products and here's why. Employees in the purchasing department often feel that their value to the organization will be measured and judged by how little they can pay for a particular product or service. Their perception of value is way too frequently driven by price rather than total overall value. *"Look at how much money I saved the company!"* is a chest-thumping cry heard in many purchasing departments. But these same people are rarely the ones who identify the high-level strategic need that evolves from recognizing a problem or issue that requires attention. With high-level purchases, that strategic investigation and subsequent problem-solving process is carried out at much higher levels – often in the C-Suite.

It's here that the most important challenges facing the organization are identified and where the framework for solutions is created. The C-Suite is the arena of forward-facing evaluation and solution architecture and it's the place where truly great sales professionals earn their stripes. In order to be effective at this level, sales professionals cannot merely be product and service vendors listing off the features and benefits of their offerings regardless of how great they may be. Instead they must be big-picture problem solvers; industry analysts who take a much broader view of the challenges facing an organization. They're experienced and trusted advisors who have the ability to provide solid advice that won't be construed as obviously self-serving. They understand that in order to create maximum value for their customers, they must recognize and appreciate the issues and concerns at the executive level.

I hope it's becoming increasingly clear to you that the time that most C-Suite executives get involved in the purchasing process is at its very genesis – at the time of early problem identification and tactical solution planning. Salespeople who don't strategically position themselves at this point, at the first emergence of the issue, rarely get on the executive radar. Perhaps executives are seeing an industry trend they feel will have a negative impact on their future revenues. Or maybe it's an opportunity they're perfectly positioned to exploit if they could just add a few more weapons to their existing arsenal. Whatever it is, it's often something that looms on the horizon rather than an existing fire that needs to be extinguished. The existing fires can be handled by lower levels of management and these situations are delegated accordingly, as they should be.

Timing is Critical

Studies show that about 80 percent of executives get involved early in the purchasing process to prioritize the project and set the vision. So it's at this time you should be working to bring the value of your products or services to the table. During the middle phase of the buying cycle, it's common for executives to limit their involvement and delegate to subordinates or committees. It's commonly the time when C-Suite executives in medium to large size companies are least likely to meet with the salesperson.

This middle stage is where most quotes or proposals are requested. The solution has already been framed and now it's off to the purchasing department where they try to find the least expensive option based on pre-set criteria. Is it any wonder why RFPs are so competitive?

It is common, however, for executives to get involved again later in the buying process to make sure the selected vendor can deliver on the value committed to. But at this point, unless you've been fortunate enough to have passed through the purchasing gauntlet and become that selected vendor, your chance at influence is gone. Even if you are the selected vendor, you've usually had to take a bit of a beating in order to reach this point. While you may still have a degree of influence over the project proceedings from this point forward, it will never be the same type of opportunity that existed at the beginning of the process. The early bird truly does have a better chance of getting the worm and that's something that should be top of mind for you.

Business Drivers for the C-Suite

At this point, I want to focus once again on the executive mindset and explore the executive decision making process and the drivers that influence those decisions.

In most of the organizations I've worked with, top level executives follow a process that, if not exactly the same, follows a format very much like this:

1. *They gain an understanding of current issues and threats*
2. *They establish vision and goals*
3. *They determine strategy and a singular focus*
4. *They explore resources and options*
5. *Vendor criteria is determined*
6. *Alternatives are explored*
7. *They plan execution and finally...*
8. *They review and measure*

But in looking between the lines and digging a bit deeper, I've been able to identify some of the common drivers that affect this entire process. When you understand what lies beneath the surface, and often really drives the decision-making process, you'll be better equipped to deliver meaningful value.

Economic Drivers

First up are *Economic Drivers*. In simple terms, executives must either produce a profit for the company or reduce costs. If executives are under financial pressure, they're being held accountable to these two high-profile measuring sticks. For you to add value, you must help them accomplish one or the other, or in the best case scenario –

both. Depending on the industry, your features and benefits must be linked to either increasing revenues or decreasing costs, or both.

Operational Drivers

Next up are *Operational Drivers*. C-Level executives are often charged with identifying areas for internal improvements and how these improvements will impact financial results. They must develop the right operational strategies, adopting the latest approaches and making sure the right people and the right technologies are available to support these strategies.

Supply Chain Drivers

Next are *Supply Chain Drivers*. Executives are often charged with ensuring the continuous supply of materials to maintain and improve production quality and to manage inventory, warehousing and distribution. The quality of their current supply chain can often either enhance or hinder the decision-making process.

Strategic Alliance Drivers

Strategic Alliance Drivers often enter the picture for many C-Level executives. They routinely look for new relationships that will further enhance or protect their current position. This represents a significant opportunity for you to increase your value offering by introducing them to other valued resources in your network.

Customer-Centric Drivers

And then there are *Customer-Centric Drivers*. Most executives are tasked with growing and insulating their existing customer base, improving loyalty and delivering value to the customer. Top sales professionals understand that if they can effectively demonstrate how their product or service will add value to the customer, then executives will listen.

Competitive Drivers

Competitive Drivers should never be overlooked. Executives can identify and understand their direct competitors, but the hidden, indirect competitors that seemingly come out of nowhere to become market leaders are tougher to spot. For example, if you had told someone in the not-too-distant past that a computer manufacturer would become the dominant force in the music distribution industry, you might have been laughed at. But that's exactly what happened with the introduction of iTunes from Apple. Because you sell your products or services to many different companies, you're in a unique position to offer insights into market trends that could have a direct impact on the executive's company.

Global Drivers

While it's not always the case, many times *Global Drivers* play a significant role. Executives understand that to remain globally competitive, they must continuously seek cost reductions in their domestic infrastructures or outsource services to low-cost providers. This carries risk and raises lots of issues, so any insights you can provide into the issues they might face would be welcomed by the C-Suite.

Compliance Drivers

Finally, *Compliance Drivers* often come into play. Whether its accounting compliance, labor laws, workplace safety, environmental regulations or even international tax rules, if you have wisdom or knowledge that will help executives stay compliant, you'll be well received at the executive level.

If you'll discipline yourself to consider the drivers that exist in the background of the executive decision-making process when you formulate your questions and subsequent presentations and proposals, you'll find in most cases that executive audiences will be far more receptive, because they'll know that you understand the type of stresses and pressures they face in the C-Suite.

What Type of Vendor are You?

As I'm sure you'd agree, selling to the C-Suite can and should involve a different process than what is typically necessary for other types of customers. The level of sophistication here is different and it means that as a sales professional hoping to gain access to this level, your sales process has to be equal to the task at hand.

Features and Benefits Based

The most common sales model used at lower levels of the organization is based on product features and benefits. Salespeople work diligently to become experts on the attributes of their own offering and then work to convince their customers that these particular features and benefits are superior to those of the competition. Unfortunately, when this is your approach, you run the risk of becoming viewed simply as a commodity vendor. Salespeople in this category see their market through a pair of product glasses. They believe that if they can just get the opportunity to demonstrate their product or service, the features and benefits, along with their company's brand, this will help them become successful. Their sales activities look like this: set up meetings, make sales presentations, give product demonstrations and write proposals.

The Product Specialist

C-Suite executives regard these salespeople merely as product specialists. They routinely refer them down to lower level staff members who deal primarily with product and technical issues. Executives don't want to deal with these salespeople themselves because their perception is that this level of salesperson is only comfortable discussing product issues.

In other words, even if, through hard work and consistent effort, the product-focused, commodity salesperson lands an initial meeting with the executive, his inability to discuss the issues that are important to the executive changes a potential opportunity into a waste of time for all parties involved. Further access to the executive is pretty much eliminated.

It simply won't cut it in the C-Suite. That's because the commodity salesperson is not focusing on what matters to senior executives. What they care about is problem solving. Their task is to find solutions to problems, not to interview product vendors. Finding a vendor to provide the required product or service needed comes after the solution is arrived at, after the strategic problem solving process is complete. By then, it's usually too late to exert any influence on senior executives. They'll have already delegated the task of vendor interviewing and selection down to a lower level of management.

If you hope to be successful at the C-Suite level, you need to enter the process during the strategic problem solving stage where you can exert a level of influence over what type of solution is arrived at. The key to selling to the executive level is to provide meaningful ideas and suggestions for the executive's business rather than simply providing a feature dump of your own product. If you show up and immediately delve into your company's features and benefits, you're virtually ensuring your own demise.

So what exactly do executives want to see? What would ensure that you'd get an audience at the C-Suite level? Well, let's take a look.

What Executives Want

First and foremost, high-level executives are looking for people who are problem solvers. Your value at this level will be determined by the extent to which you can position yourself as a high-level problem solver. Executives are looking for salespeople that can speak their language, have an understanding of their corporate strategy and can add value to their business. You've got to shift your focus from your own products to a broader view that encompasses the bigger picture your customers face with their businesses. Your ideas and suggestions must be more strategically focused on industry positioning – right now and especially for the future. Problem solving salespeople seek to understand their customers' business challenges and then work to provide creative solutions to those problems. If your answers can be seen as serving the executive's best interests rather than being transparently self-serving, then you'll change the executive's perception of what type of value you bring to the table.

The Strategic Resource

You're now evolving from a salesperson to a *strategic resource*. A salesperson who has evolved from a commodity provider to a strategic resource is in a unique position to get involved in the decision making process. Strategic resource providers stand out from commodity providers because they have done their homework and can identify what needs to be accomplished in order for their customers to achieve preferred status in their marketplaces. When you can articulate a desirable destination and describe the steps needed to get there, then purchasing the products you represent will seem like a natural progression in a bigger strategic plan for the C-Suite executive. You often don't even need to *sell* them. When presented effectively, the executive often will say something like, *"That makes really good sense to me. Now, how can we get this done? Do you have what we need to make this happen?"* At this point, you can start bringing your product and service offering to the forefront. And take note – there's a big difference – it comes *after* the solution is arrived at. You never lead with products and services right out of the gate or as we've discussed previously, you'll simply be viewed as a product-focused, commodity salesperson.

Trusted Advisor

If you can produce as promised, you now start to progress to the next level; to that of *trusted advisor*. With experience and consistent production, you can become an inner confidant; someone the executive will be willing to bring into the inner circle to offer insight and advice on industry direction. As a trusted advisor, you routinely offer suggestions on industry challenges, provide insight into best practices and help companies steer clear of the potholes in the road they may not be able to see, but that you do because of your unique perspective.

Trusted advisors understand the personal agendas of their customers and find ways to leverage their own company's resources to deliver complete solutions. They offer personal value as well as applicable commercial value. It's critical for trusted advisors to understand the issues the executives are dealing with and help them establish objectives for their business agendas – again, always before identifying the capabilities their own companies provide. This is how you build relationships with C-Suite executives.

Relevant Contact

Before we go any further, there's one very important thing to note here and that's to ensure that you're always trying to get in touch with the right executive. You can actually do more harm than good if you call on executives just because they appear to be at the top of the food chain. The key is not to just find an executive but rather to find the relevant executive. Relevant means this person is the one responsible for the problem that you can solve and that can have an impact on your compensation. Ideally, the relevant executives are the ones who have a mix of internal rank and influence as well as the authority to initiate projects and find the necessary funding. They must have the authority to marshal internal resources that support the overall corporate strategy.

They have reach not just in their own silos, but across many different departments. It's also important to note that the relevant executives are not always in the C-Suite and if you inadvertently go over their heads you may be alienating yourself before you ever get started. So make sure you do a bit of research and find out as much as you can to make sure you're approaching the correct person; the one who'll actually be calling the shots. To find out who that person is, make sure you ask yourself these two questions:

1. *Who would be the person to set the strategic direction that would result in an eventual purchase decision?*
2. *Who has the greatest influence?*

Once you've found out exactly who will be the most strategic contact in the organization for you, you'll be ready to start formulating your specific access strategy.

Gaining Access

Gaining access is often the most difficult aspect of selling to the C-Suite. It can be intimidating for the sales rookie and often still represents a very real test to highly experienced salespeople. There's no doubt that access at this level is not as simple as sending out an introductory email and asking for an appointment.

Referrals and Recommendations

Let's start with the most effective strategy of them all. And that's through a recommendation from someone who works at the prospective executive's company. Put simply, internal recommendations or referrals carry the most weight. If you already have a relationship with someone in your target organization, try to use their relationship leverage to open the door for you. A good word from an internal source is often just the advantage you need to secure that initial briefing.

Many times, however, that isn't possible and it becomes necessary for you to navigate past the corporate roadblocks that exist in most organizations. But just remember, these roadblocks aren't erected to make the salesperson's job more difficult. They're put in place so the executive can focus on important tasks and not be distracted. They exist because far too many salespeople are time wasters that haven't done their homework and don't know how to position value that will make sense at the executive level.

The Executive Assistant

The first and often biggest hurdle is the executive assistant who serves as the main gatekeeper. In many cases, it's impossible to get face time with your target executive unless you first connect with the executive assistant. So don't try to evade or ignore them. Instead, engage them! Make it part of your overall strategy to treat gatekeepers as if they actually were the executives. Explain your distinctive value proposition to them and ask for their opinions. Many times, these gatekeepers understand their executive's business issues and will recognize the value you bring to the table. Always keep this good rule of thumb in mind: if the gatekeeper helps you, thank them and always keep them in the loop!

The amount of time you spend in getting to know a bit more about the gatekeeper will often pay huge dividends. They're almost always in the positions they have because they're highly trusted by the executives they serve. So logically, it follows that if you can get a recommendation from the executive assistant, you're much more likely to get your foot in the door.

A great way to make your initial introduction is call and ask for the executive assistant. In most cases they are highly accessible. Your call might go something like this:

"Hello Ms. Anderson, thank you for taking my call. My name is Michael Vickers and I work for ABC Communications. Part of my role at ABC is to brief retail industry executives (or whatever niche you are targeting) *on the latest innovations and strategies in communications*

and what trends we see happening in their specific industries. I under-
stand that you work directly with Mr. Palmer and I assume that he has
a busy schedule and I was hoping you could guide me to the best way
for me to connect with him. I'm looking for about 20 minutes and I
think Mr. Palmer will find the conversation useful. Then if there is any
further interest, Mr. Palmer can send me to the appropriate contact in
your organization."

During your conversation with the executive assistant, take the opportunity to bring him or her into the loop about some of the things you would want to brief the target executive on. If it's valid information that he or she can readily see would be important or interesting to the executive, you'll have a much better chance of gaining access.

Executive Contact

So let's assume that you've passed the gatekeeper hurdle and are now ready for your first contact with your target executive. Your first goal should always be to set up a briefing meeting. It's often the most difficult part of the selling process because executives are not yet aware of any value you may represent to them and their normal first reaction is to deflect sales overtures to others in the organization. So your first contact must provide a clue as to the value you represent and that it's value that is meaningful to those at the executive level.

Once you connect with the executive, the conversation might go like this:

"Hello Mr. Palmer. My name is Michael Vickers and I work for ABC
Communications here in Dallas. Part of my role at ABC is to brief
retail industry executives on the latest innovations and strategies in
communications and what trends are impacting their businesses. I'm
not sure yet if we have anything to be talking about Mr. Palmer, that's
why I'm calling. With your permission, I would like to schedule a
20-minute briefing with you to meet you personally, show you how

*other companies in the retail industry are employing these technol-
ogies and then make a determination if there is anything we should
be talking about."*

So now let's break this down and see how the structure of the call works.

Setting the Stage

The first thing you're doing is *setting the stage*. The first 30 seconds
are critical when you make an initial approach to an executive. You
want to be perceived as prepared and confident. The goal of this call
is to build enough interest to establish an executive briefing.

Your introduction should identify your position in your organization and clearly communicate that your role is to brief executives
on new developments, strategies and technologies available in the
marketplace that will help them either generate revenue, reduce
costs, improve productivity or increase customer satisfaction; all
things that are extremely important at this level.

Be sure to state your purpose. Remember, the purpose of the call is
to set up a briefing – that's it. We still aren't talking solutions at this
point, so there should be no conversation regarding any of your products or services. Later, at the briefing, you can determine if there is
more that you should be discussing.

Establishing Credibility

You should also be working to establish credibility in your introductory contact. In your first brief moments, let the executive know
that you have done your homework on the organization, re-affirm the
value you can deliver and describe how you have helped other companies in the segment with similar challenges. If you've been referred
by someone, you can use this source to vouch for your credibility.

Make sure you're very clear of what your intentions are and what
you think the next step should be. If it makes sense to the executive,
they will grant you the briefing. One possibility at this point is that you

may get referred to someone lower in the organization. This is not the most desired result, but it can still be productive. Ask the executive for an introduction to the person so that you don't have to call them cold. Ask the executive if he or she has an expected outcome from your meeting with this next contact and if there's anything to follow up on. Finally, ask to reconnect with the executive after you have met with the referred contact to keep the executive in the loop.

The Briefing Meeting

At this point, I'll assume that you've been successful in securing the briefing meeting and are now ready to meet with the C-Suite executive. You've done all your relevant homework and should be prepared with both the information you want to share, as well as a list of high-value questions that will spur conversations and identify the best opportunities for you. As we discussed earlier in creating your Question Protocol, remember that your questions shouldn't be focused simply around your own products and services. They must be framed around the executive's business and industry; questions that show an understanding of their issues and concerns. They're bigger picture inquiries that spur conversation about the things that matter most at the executive level – market growth, revenue generation, operational efficiency, customer retention and future opportunities. Salespeople who follow a well-structured Question Protocol will bring new perspectives and will add value to the organization. To help you generate your questions and frame your presentation at the briefing, let's take a look at a few things most executives are almost always looking for.

1. *Ways to increase revenues and reduce costs.*

2. *Ways to increase the efficiencies and effectiveness of revenue generating employees, mission critical employees, customer facing processes and operations.*

3. *Ways to avoid unpredictable expenses.*

4. *Ways to stay compliant. Staying on the right side of rules and regulations is always of key importance.*

You already have quite a few things in common with the executive such as revenue generation and resource management, as well as cost and time containment. All of these are important to both of your positions and will give you points of similarity that you should be able to leverage.

At the Briefing

When you arrive at your meeting, keep these following pointers in mind to make sure your briefing brings the kind of results you're looking for.

Make a Good First Impression – Ensure that you're dressed and personally groomed in a manner that says you belong at this level and are comfortable interacting here. The rule of thumb is simple; the more your clothing style matches that of the executive, the more likely he or she will be to respond to your message. Whenever you're meeting with an executive, it's often a good idea to call their assistant ahead of time and ask what the executive typically wears to the office, and then mirror that style of dress. Make it a rule to dress to your audience or one step above it.

Understand their Business Goals – Seek first to understand, then seek to be understood is the mantra for all great salespeople.

Listen, Listen and Listen – Listen to what they say, listen to what they feel and listen for what they need before suggesting a solution.

Communication Skills Matter – What you say and how you say it matters. Avoid using slang or curse words, even if you hear them from your executive counterpart, but you should try to incorporate words and phrases that the executive uses and understands. As you work within a specific segment, you will notice the language nuances are similar within industries.

Provide Industry Insights & Wisdom – Sales professionals who can provide insights at the industry level will engender the respect and trust of senior executives.

Avoid Your Own Industry Speak and Jargon – Don't use acronyms or language that the executive doesn't know or won't recognize. It doesn't make you sound informed and it can be construed as a direct challenge to the executive's ego, power and authority. Use words and language the executive will be familiar with.

Demonstrate your Accountability – Executives love to have a single source of accountability. They want to know you'll be responsible for the success or failure of the project. Make sure they know that you're the go-to person that can make things happen for them.

Respect the Executive's Time – Executives take their time seriously. They are driven to achieve their goals and objectives and anything that delays them from their daily achievements becomes an interruption.

After the Briefing

Once you've completed your briefing interview, you'll more than likely have some things you'll need to follow up on. If there appears to be the possibility of a sale in the near future, be sure to try to schedule a follow-up meeting or at the very least, let the executive know when you're planning to get in touch with them again. Then make sure you do it as scheduled! As I alluded to earlier, accountability is extremely important at this level. When you make contact again, you can position the benefits of your products or services directly around the executive's stated needs and business concerns.

Even if there doesn't appear to be an imminent sale on the horizon, you'll still want to position yourself for future opportunities. A great way to do this is to suggest that you include the executive on future dispatches that you regularly send to high-level clients to keep them abreast of the latest developments in their industries. This keeps your name in front of them and attached to valuable information that impacts their business. These dispatches can come in the form of emails, white papers, business blogs, seminars or whatever you use to disseminate information to your clients. Just make sure that it's always seen as coming from you personally and it's not just a generic mail-out intended for any level of customer. It must be tailored toward the executive customer and be focused on value as they perceive value. It should never appear to be just a product flyer or you'll lose your C-Suite audience in a hurry.

Let the executive receive a few of these regularly scheduled update dispatches and then schedule a follow-up call to see how his business is going and if there are any new needs or concerns that might be able to be addressed with your company's offering. Timing for your follow-up calls is important – you don't want to be perceived as a pest – so if you tell your client that your protocol with C-Suite executives is to follow-up quarterly to check in and keep in touch, then I think you'll find that most executives won't see 4 times a year as overly bothersome.

What's Next

We've covered a lot of ground to this point and you may be asking yourself how in the world you're going to find the time to manage and implement all the strategies you've learned. Well, fear not, because that's exactly what we'll be covering in our next chapter. I'll introduce you to a new model for managing your time; one that's tailor-made for today's busy Rainmaker. I'm confident that upon inspection, you'll agree it makes a lot more sense than the model so many sales professionals are still using by default today.

CHAPTER 11

The 21st Century Time System

To be successful in today's hyper-competitive marketplace, it's essential that sales professionals maximize their productivity. That's often easier said than done, especially when we have a lifetime of habits that have been ingrained into our daily routines. The 21st Century Time System is designed to increase productivity by changing the way you look at managing your time and allowing you to focus your efforts on revenue-generating activities in a way that can be effectively maintained over the long term.

Throughout this chapter, we'll examine the simple changes you can make to dramatically increase your productivity while still striking a balance that will enable you to maintain your effectiveness in the long run.

An Outdated Time System

The North American work week we've come to know typically runs from Monday to Friday, from 9am to 5pm, but it certainly wasn't always like this. In the Agricultural Age, work was done when it needed to be done and it wasn't until the evolution of the Industrial Age that the concept of a shorter work week came into existence with the need for a break from the long hours of manufacturing, for family and personal time. The 7-day work week of the Agricultural Age evolved to 5 days of work followed by 2 days of downtime at week's end. This is the work/time system we still see in place in most work environments today.

In the typical Monday to Friday, 9 to 5 system, the default method of time management involves trying to accomplish a wide variety of tasks each day of the week. As our lives become busier and more complex with so many things to do, only a small amount of time can be devoted to each individual task. As a result, we often become over-whelmed and experience a great deal of frustration at not being able to accomplish as much as we would like. We suffer through 5 days of this and then we thankfully arrive at the weekend when we can stop the madness for a couple of days only to start up again on Monday. Is it any wonder that studies show people are 20% more likely to suffer heart attacks on Mondays than any other day of the week? Talk about a never-ending merry-go-round! Yet most people still continue with this model even though they know it's not producing the results they want, simply because they don't know how to do things differently.

While the Monday to Friday work week is still very much in exis-tence, today's advances in technology are allowing people to work in a much wider array of locations, and as a result, flexible work schedules are becoming increasingly common. In addition, the pace of work has accelerated due to the global nature of today's marketplace. It's clear that the workplace is going through another major evolution. To stay on top, it's vital that today's Rainmakers adjust to the new pace of the workplace.

Your Operating System

A helpful metaphor is to think of our current time system as a com-puter operating system. As computer hardware evolves and capabilities increase, computer operating systems must be upgraded to take advan-tage of new capabilities, to increase efficiencies and to pave the way for subsequent software development. Old operating systems weren't designed for the new hardware and software so they can't possibly be expected to work efficiently. It only makes sense to upgrade.

The same logic applies to time management. We need to upgrade today if we hope to increase efficiencies and stay current with the market. While this may seem obvious, the truth is that most sales professionals still operate with old mindsets. In fact, the 21st Century Time System can be, by itself, a point of competitive differentiation just because so few people employ it. In other words, if you will incorporate this new system into your work routines, you will become more productive than your competitor in the same amount of time. And that's because the 21st Century Time System is not about working harder, it's about working smarter; working smarter so that you can be more successful in a rapidly changing marketplace while still maintaining a healthy balance between work and life.

New Terminology

The first thing you'll need to learn is a bit of new terminology. Once you're familiar with the definitions of the terms you'll learn in the 21st Century Time System, we can move on to application strategies.

The system is broken down into specific types of days and types of time.

Rainmaker Day

The first type of day is what I call a *Rainmaker Day*. A Rainmaker Day is one where 80% of your time is specifically focused on money-making activities. This is the day where you go full-out, hitting on all cylinders. In sports, we call it *Game Day*. This is what you practice and prepare for.

It means that if you work an 8 hour day, 6.5 hours are spent on activities that directly generate revenue for you and your company. It is important that the results generated from these activities will have a direct impact on generating sales revenue.

Examples of these activities might be:

- Meeting with your best clients – the best being the top 20%.
- Meeting with new prospects or customers.
- Presenting your solutions and making prospecting telephone calls, closing deals or generating new ones.

Any activity that directly generates revenue can count as a Rainmaker Day activity.

Maintenance Day

Maintenance Days are cleanup and preparation days. On a Maintenance Day, we write proposals, prepare quotes, send thank you notes, return phone calls and we can even make sales calls and close deals. Any day where we spend *less* than 80% of our time on money-making activities is a Maintenance Day. Even if you land a big sale, it's still a Maintenance Day and not a Rainmaker Day if you've spent less than 80% of your day on direct money-making activities. For the vast majority of sales professionals, the Maintenance Day is the day-to-day norm and up until this point, it's probably been your norm as well.

Rejuvenation Day

The third type of day is the *Rejuvenation Day*. Even though it sounds less important than a Rainmaker or Maintenance Day, make no mistake, it's of equal importance – especially long term. Rejuvenation Days are free of work. That basically means no business related activities. No checking emails on your smart phone, no business conversations with colleagues or clients – unless of course it's an emergency, but those rarely, if ever, occur.

It's vital that you treat Rejuvenation Days seriously. Study after study on the subject of productivity demonstrates that your ability to achieve a productive Rainmaker Day is directly proportionate to your ability to rejuvenate. We need our downtime. Without downtime, our capacity for productivity on a daily basis is diminished because we're operating at an unacceptable level of fatigue. Over the long term, we subject ourselves to the very real risk of burnout.

Rejuvenation days are about spending time with family and friends or for time just for yourself. They're about reconnecting with what's important in your life on the personal side. Real success is only achieved by reaching a healthy sense of balance. So there's no need to feel guilty about taking time off. It's absolutely necessary if you're going to make the 21st Century Time System work for you.

Creativity Day

The fourth and final type of day in our system is the *Creativity Day*. Creativity days can occur whenever they're necessary or when the creative muse awakens within, but you should never just leave them to chance. New ideas are the lifeblood of all business and represent the greatest opportunity for healthier margins. Clients will pay more for an idea that is fresh and new and not being implemented by anyone else. When there is nothing to compare it to, you can set the pricing to reflect the true worth of the idea. Unfortunately, if the idea is strong enough, it's bound to be copied. The window for higher margins will close as the competition catches up and introduces a *me too* version. At that point, pricing pressure comes into play and margins shrink. So creativity is vital to your bottom line and should be planned for accordingly. Ideally, once a quarter, you should reserve one day for High Touch and Distinctive Value idea generation. That means you have one day a quarter to plan creative ways to enhance your top economic relationships. Questions to ask on this day are:

- *What can I do for my top business clients from a "High Touch" point of view?*
- *Is there anything I'm currently doing that I can up-level to a point where my client will say, "Wow, I certainly didn't expect that!"?*

In essence, Creativity Days help to keep you focused on continuous improvement and give you an opportunity to work on your business rather than just in it.

R&D Time

Our first time strategy is what we call *R&D Time*, and as you are probably already aware, R&D stands for Research and Development.

It should come as no surprise that companies that are adept in the area of research and development have a very tangible advantage over companies that don't. Although research and development can be expensive and time consuming, the results can reap benefits for years to come. Companies that continuously out-perform the competition invariably have strong research and development capabilities and they're constantly working at developing what's coming next to ensure they stay ahead of the pack.

If this is true for corporations, it can also be true for individual business professionals as well. As a Rainmaker, how much time do you set aside for personal research and development? Your research could be focused on new approaches or techniques; perhaps it might involve seeking out best practices in your industry. When was the last time you learned and tried new techniques or processes? Research and development does take time – make no mistake. And we often hear from sales professionals that time is the big problem. They don't have the time for research and development. They're just too busy with their day-to-day activities. Yet these same people often have no trouble managing to squeeze in some time to read the morning newspaper. For many people, reading the morning paper is an ingrained ritual that gets their day started by getting them in a *thinking* frame of mind. They're right – the morning is the best time to learn. We're more open to intellectual challenges when we're fresh and rested. If we wait until the end of the day, our minds are often exhausted and a good dose of research will put us to sleep.

With the 21st Century Time System, the morning paper ritual is changed to R&D Time. When you get in the habit of reading with a business purpose first thing in the morning, your perspective and outlook will change and your results will start to reflect your increased level of knowledge.   A good tip is to catch up on current events after work. Read fiction at night, on weekends or holidays and read your business material as early as possible in the day. A good business book or business-related article will put money in your pocket – a newspaper won't, unless you use it for prospecting purposes, in which case avoid reading the negative articles.

Power Break Time

My definition of *Power Break Time* is 20 to 30 minutes of disengage time every day, particularly on Rainmaker or Maintenance days. Power Break Time is just simply a break in your full-out schedule. Think of it as an intermission at halftime. Most professional sports allow these 20-minute breaks to rejuvenate, re-think and basically recharge batteries before the game resumes. If they're useful and productive for professional athletes, they'll have a tremendous benefit for high-performing Rainmakers as well.

Applying the System

To illustrate the 21st Century Time System in action, let me show you how I apply it to enhance my own productivity.

Saturday

Unlike most conventional business calendars, my work week starts on a Saturday. That's Day 1 for me. Saturdays are generally free for me because most people don't go to seminars or conferences on the weekend, so it's ideal. Each industry or business will have its ideal slow days – you can figure out which works best for you. Saturdays for me are an excellent Rejuvenation Day. That means I don't do any business-related work on those days. I don't do proposals, emails, or anything that even looks like business-related work. Besides being great for your relationships with your partner and children, it's also good for your own personal morale.

Too often, sales professionals get up on Saturday morning and get started on paperwork. They'll check their emails and contemplate their past business week and the one coming up. Instead of rejuvenating, their minds are kicked into work mode again. That's a no-no on a Rejuvenation Day within the 21st Century Time System.

The quality of your Rainmaker Days is directly proportional to the quality of your Rejuvenation Days. Even highly-trained professional athletes, whose fitness is tremendously accelerated, know they must take days off during the week to rest their muscles and recuperate fully. To do otherwise is to court injury and burnout.

What you end up doing on your Rejuvenation Day is ultimately up to you, but I always recommend something physical or exercise-related to remove any stress that has been accumulating.

Sunday

Sunday is another day that is easy to dedicate to rejuvenation. Rarely, if ever, do I have a business seminar or workshop that has been scheduled for a Sunday. On most Sundays, I get to hang out with my family, but every once in a while, I do have to travel to another city for a Monday presentation or sales call. On the days that I have to travel for business, I usually combine a little paperwork as well. That changes it from a Rejuvenation Day to a Maintenance Day. Because I've lost a Rejuvenation Day in this scenario, it's important that I get in another makeup Rejuvenation Day as soon as possible. If I use up a Rejuvenation Day on the weekend for work, I will often pick up a Friday or some other day the following week as a substitution.

Monday

Now when Monday rolls around, I am usually ready to start my work week. It's not usually a Rainmaker day for me, but under certain circumstances, it might be. One of the great things about the 21st Century Time System is that it allows you to maintain enough flexibility to react to circumstances as they arise. In most cases, I use Monday as a Maintenance Day to clean up any outstanding issues from the prior week and to prepare for the rest of the coming week. I still may make a few sales calls and possibly prepare proposals and complete agreements. I might have lunch with a colleague and for sure, a visit to the gym. It's pretty much a normal work day for me.

Tuesday

Tuesday is a Rainmaker Day for me. It's game day and I'm firing on all cylinders. Based on our definition of what a Rainmaker Day is, my goal is to spend 80% of my time on revenue-producing activities. For me, that means presenting or training or meeting with high-revenue or high-potential clients. Any activity that directly contributes to generating revenue can be included as part of my Rainmaker Day. And it's all about generating and sustaining momentum. If I close a sale on a Rainmaker Day, I don't stop to tie up all the loose ends. I just leave them and move on to the next revenue generating activity. This is an important detail to remember as most salespeople don't work this way. Often, on the day a sale is closed, salespeople let out a whoop of joy or maybe a sigh of relief and then promptly take their foot of the gas. They'll linger on the great feeling of closing the sale and then tidy up the paperwork and make sure everything is in order for that particular client. Well, that's a real momentum killer. The best time for you to close the next sale is right after you've closed the previous one! You're on a roll – don't stop, keep the momentum rolling. Go right after another. With the 21st Century Time System, you don't worry about the follow-up details on a Rainmaker Day. A Rainmaker Day is all about going full-out and keeping your mojo and confidence at a high level.

In sports, athletes relish those all too rare times when they enter what they call *the zone*. When an athlete is in the zone, everything is clear and what is often very difficult, suddenly becomes easy. There's a tremendous surge of confidence and a feeling of invincibility. You want it to last as long as possible and you know that the only way to keep it going is to have laser-like focus and maintain concentration. But the zone can be a fragile and elusive state. Sometimes the smallest distraction can take you out and then it's really hard to get back in it.

It should be the same way for sales professionals on a Rainmaker Day. You want to get in the zone and then stay totally focused and ride the wave as long as you can. The details can wait. Take your next shot right away. Keep your concentration and focus strong and block out distractions. Rainmaker Days are mentally and physically demanding and that's just the way they should be. I start early and go full-out throughout the day and by the end of the day I'm usually pretty tired, but I know I've achieved a lot. You get a real sense of satisfaction and accomplishment at the end of a great Rainmaker Day. If you're still struggling a bit to envision a Rainmaker Day for yourself, think of what your day is like before you leave to go on a vacation. You're hustling to get everything done and there's a real sense of urgency in your work. You don't have time to go to lunch with buddies – you're just too busy. You're focused on getting things done – client meetings, sales calls and getting everything organized because there's no time to do it tomorrow. This is what a Rainmaker Day should feel like.

Wednesday, Thursday and Friday

The day following a Rainmaker Day is a bit more relaxed for me. It's a Maintenance Day. With my schedule, I follow a Rainmaker Tuesday with a Maintenance Day Wednesday. It's the day after game day. I have lots of cleanup from the day before and as we've talked about, that's just the way I want it. On Maintenance Days, I take care of the details and then spend some time prepping for my Thursday, because on Thursday, I'm back in high gear for another Rainmaker Day.

Friday is another Maintenance Day, again to clean up any loose ends from Thursday, attend to office necessities and prepare for up-coming sales activities.

That cycles me back into the weekend to start a new week. Now you'll notice in my example, I only schedule two Rainmaker Days in a week. It's been my experience that just two Rainmaker Days per week are enough to greatly improve your sales performance. Any more than that and you risk burnout over the long haul. It's just not feasible to expect to deliver Rainmaker Day after Rainmaker Day. But scheduling 2 per week with Maintenance Days in between is usually sustainable for high-performing salespeople.

Annual Numbers

On an annual basis, this system will give you at least 100 Rain-maker Days a year and that's a busy schedule. Professional athletes in high-energy sports such as hockey and basketball have about 80 games per year not including pre-season and playoffs, so you're in the same ballpark as other peak performing professionals.

The reason this system is so effective for sales professionals is that, based upon our research, the average sales professional has only about 20 to 30 days a year that are the equivalent of our Rainmaker Days. Most salespeople operate with a week full of what we define as Maintenance Days.

Even if you start with only one Rainmaker Day per week, you'll still achieve a significant boost in overall annual productivity compared to the average sales professional. That boost will yield results that you can take to the bank!

Planning and Priorities

Sales professionals know that not all prospects and customers are created equal. Some have terrific potential and represent significant value to us and our companies, while others are high maintenance time-suckers that never yield the kind of results we're hoping for. The key to greater success then often comes down to your ability to determine which is which and your decisions about who is most worthy of your efforts and resources.

The Pareto Principle

As discussed earlier, the Pareto Principle, which is commonly known as the 80/20 rule, states that 80% of your sales will come from about 20% of your customers. As you drill down further and really examine your sales results, you'll more than likely find that about 50% of your business actually comes from about 5% of your customers. Finally, you'll probably discover that about 10% of your customers provide all the net profit for the company.

So here's a rule of thumb to help you understand what all of these figures mean to you. As a sales professional, you should spend about 50% of your selling time or Rainmaker activities on high-potential accounts, which translates into about 5-20% of your account base. The remaining 50% of your time can be devoted to everyone else.

So right about now you may be wondering, "How do I accurately determine a high-potential account? With so many opportunities available to me, how do I determine which opportunities are going to get my limited time and energy? What's the best way to measure an account's potential?" These are great questions and every Rainmaker should be able to answer them.

Focusing on the Right Things

Many salespeople make the strategic mistake of focusing on accounts that will generate the most revenue for their company. In other words, for them, potential is measured solely by the dollars earned. There is another variable, however, that should be factored in before making that determination. That factor is *time*. Potential is really the ratio of dollars earned to the amount of time invested to realize those dollars. The formula illustrated is:

$$\frac{\text{Potential Revenue}}{\text{Time Invested}} = \text{Real Potential}$$

So it's not about how much a customer will buy from you, it's how much will they buy from you in relation to the amount of time you must invest in them.

Making a Choice

Let me give you an example to illustrate this. In my example, I'm looking at 2 different companies with good potential, but I only have the time to go after one at this particular point. I've got to decide which one is going to be my main priority. I've determined that ABC Company represents a potential of $50,000 in revenue, but will probably require 100 hours of time to make it happen. My other prospect, XYZ Company represents less potential revenue, about $20,000, but needs only 20 hours of time. Both decent prospects, but who should I go after? Let's apply our formula to this situation.

For ABC Company, we'll take the potential revenue of $50,000 and divide it by the 100 hours of time needed to bring it to fruition. That gives us a real potential number of 500. For XYZ Company, we'll take our $20,000 potential revenue figure and divide it by the 20 hours needed to complete the sale. The result is a real potential number of 1000. Using our formula, it's clear that XYZ Company has *double* the real potential. Here's how to think of this... I would need 100 hours to land $50,000 worth of business if I focused on this category of client. If I invest 100 hours in the XYZ category of clients, I would generate $100,000 worth of business.

Time and Money

Time and money go hand-in-hand and you only have a finite number of hours to invest. Smart Rainmakers will do the math and make sure they're investing their time with potential clients that represent the best real potential from a big picture point of view. Using our formula to determine high potential accounts is a good example of a planning discipline I call *Analyze then Prioritize*. Carefully examining the tasks that you have to perform as a sales professional will allow you to prioritize them much more effectively. So how can we best analyze and prioritize our activities? Are there some sales activities that are of higher priority than others? How do we determine their importance? What is the best way to prioritize your clients and opportunities?

7 Steps to More Effective Planning

The 21st Century Time System can really be leveraged if you become a master planner. With that in mind, I've put together 7 steps that will really help you to become a master planner and to stay focused. Let's take a look.

1. **Constantly Re-Prioritize.** Rainmakers understand that business is dynamic and that priorities are fluid and change all the time. Daily and weekly reviews of your activities and opportunities will help you make sure you stay on track and are working on the right things at the right time.

2. **Stay Close to the Money.** This isn't as easy as it sounds, but if you work diligently and stay close to the money, you will at least be on the right side of the fence. Your job as a Rainmaker is to generate revenue for you and your company. Any task that will bring you a step closer to getting the money in hand should be high on your priority list. And that doesn't just mean making more sales calls. It might involve making a call to a client to follow-up on an outstanding invoice. Make sure you're aware of how the money flows and how you can be an enabler in that process. By staying close to the money, you ensure the organization has cash flow and that you receive a commission check.

3. **Prepare for Uncontrolled Downtime.** There are many things

that can cause your day to go sideways. Meetings get cancelled, equipment breaks, people don't show up on time; there are a myriad of possibilities. Stuff happens! And you'll significantly improve your personal productivity if you simply plan for these possibilities. Keep a list with you of top prospects you could call if you get hit with unexpected downtime. Perhaps you have a number of articles or letters you could write if your lunch appointment doesn't show up or you're stuck in a waiting room. Having a good audio business book that you can listen to in your car is also helpful if you are stuck in traffic. It's great research and development time. You'll find that if you've planned for it, downtime isn't the annoying disappointment that it was in the past.

4. **To React or Not to React?** Many salespeople feel that it's their sworn duty to react every time a customer makes a request. Now, don't get me wrong, I think it's essential to provide great customer service, however it should have its limits. Just because a customer is calling you doesn't mean you have to call them back immediately. Try leaving a message on your voice mail that tells your clients that you're working in the field today. Explain that their calls are important to you, and that you will call them back at the end of the day. If it's an emergency, have them call your sales support to handle the issue, otherwise you'll return their calls within a few hours. Not responding immediately to every request will improve your sanity and your productivity.

5. **Qualify and Prioritize Every Opportunity.** This is a very important strategy that will dramatically improve your productivity. First of all, it's essential that you fully qualify every opportunity and that you're realistic in your expectations. Qualifying them means that you don't overestimate their potential and that they have a very real possibility of becoming a customer.

6. **It's OK to Say No.** Believe it or not, sometimes you'll have to tell a customer no. *"No, we can't do that"*, *"No, I know that won't*

fly with my manager", *"No, we can't lower our pricing on that product"*, *"No, we can't meet that specification"* or, *"No, we can't make your timelines"*. I'm sure you can think of a few others. While we should always try to create a positive experience when dealing with our customers and do our best to meet their requests, it's also okay to set boundaries with some customers. A quick and effective way to do that is to allow yourself to simply say no when it's necessary.

7. **Am I Doing the Most Productive Thing I Can be Doing Right Now?** This is a great mantra for any sales professional. Say this to yourself on a regular basis and it will kick into your subconscious every time you have a spare moment. Often there are distractions that creep into our daily routine and take us away from our goals and objectives for the day. Asking this question periodically will cause you to examine your current activity and give you a chance to re-evaluate.

Plan for Disruption

Keep in mind, that no matter how well you plan, you can count on the fact that things rarely go exactly as planned. Rainmakers understand this reality and adapt accordingly. Flexibility is an important character trait of high-level Rainmakers, but if you start off with a plan first and then learn to be flexible to changing circumstances, you'll find that you'll make real gains in your planning and prioritizing effectiveness. Managing your time to keep up with today's fast-moving marketplace is imperative if you're going to enjoy the success of a true Rainmaker. The 21st Century Time System was developed to maximize the most precious resource available to you – your time. It gives you the flexibility to rejuvenate and plan for the future while effectively doubling your sales productivity if you apply it as we've described. Give yourself the gift of time and you'll be well on your way to becoming a high-performing Rainmaker.

Final Thoughts

As you come to the end of the book, it's a good time to take stock of where you've been and what still needs to be done in order to cement your status as a Rainmaker. Throughout each of the preceding chapters, I've provided you with tried, true and tested strategies to become more effective in your sales efforts; to become a Rainmaker. I know these strategies work because I've used them successfully myself as have many sales professionals across North America that I've had the pleasure to work with. They've helped low-performing salespeople break out of ruts and jump-start their careers and have helped high-performers break through ceilings to reach extraordinary new levels of performance.

But still, the knowledge I've shared with you throughout these pages does not guarantee success. Ultimately, it will be up to you to implement what you've learned, to put your newfound knowledge into action. That means effort. Effort on an ongoing basis. Trial and error, tenacity and resilience. Applying what you learn and not being afraid to struggle a bit at first and adjust as you forge ahead. Because at the end of the day, there's no magic button to push that will make things easy and effortless; it takes commitment. Your ultimate success is up to you. I've worked with thousands of salespeople just like you and the ones that make lasting changes to their organizations and their own careers through my programs all have one thing in common. They execute what they learn.

Action fuels their success. It's not enough to simply understand con-cepts; in order to create change you must take action.

The fact that you've come this far and are reading this right now tells me you have what it takes to make a difference in your company and in your own career. Great things can happen if you're willing to make that commitment and put in the effort that it takes. If you'll do that, then you'll have truly mastered the Dance of the Rainmaker.